Momma Dean's
Southern Cooking
at Meador Homestead

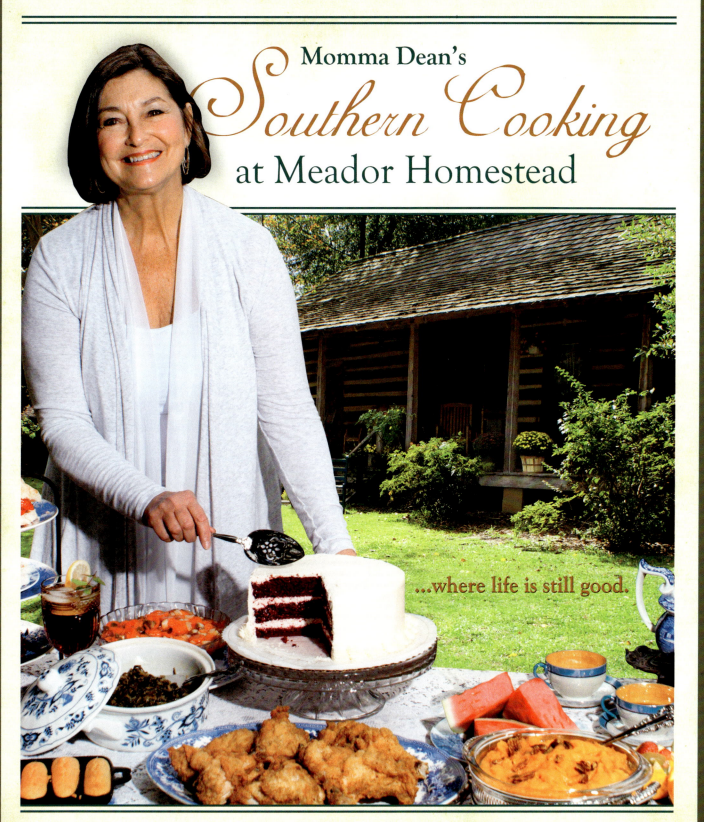

Momma Dean's
Southern Cooking
at Meador Homestead

...where life is still good.

Dean Meador Smith

Momma Dean's Southern Cooking at Meador Homestead…where life is still good

Copyright © 2012 Dean Meador Smith

All rights reserved. No portion of this publication may be reproduced, stored in a retrieval system, or transmitted by any means—electronic, mechanical, photocopying, recording, or any other—except for brief quotations in printed reviews, without the prior written permission of the publisher.

Cover & Jacket Design: Jason Kauffmann / Firelight Interactive / firelightinteractive.com

Front Cover Photographs: Corey Lunsford

Back Cover Drawing: Janet Payne Walker

Interior Design: Michael Covington

Interior Editing: Adam Tillinghast & Donna Melillo

Photography: Eddie and Dean Smith, Adams Garner, Joanna Holbert, (Chi Omega Sorority picture from McCain Library and Archives, University of Southern Mississippi), Michael Covington

Quotations and Writings: C. G. Meador (Pa), excerpt from *Stepping Heavenward* by Mrs. E. Prentiss, the poem "Walk the Woods" by Glen Smith, song "Evening in December" by Tricia Walker of Big Front Productions, Levi Parks Meador's license to preach in the Methodist Episcopal Church South, Methodist minister Pierce Harris, Pauline Smith (Eddie's mom), Wyse.

Indigo River Publishing
3 West Garden Street Ste. 352
Pensacola, FL 32502
www.indigoriverpublishing.com

Ordering Information:
Quantity sales: Special discounts are available on quantity purchases by corporations, associations, and others. For details, contact the publisher at the address above.

Orders by U.S. trade bookstores and wholesalers: Please contact the publisher at the address above.

Printed in the United States of America

Publisher's Cataloging-in-Publication Data is available upon request.

978-0-9856033-2-8

First Edition

With Indigo River Publishing, you can always expect great books, strong voices, and meaningful messages. Most importantly, you'll always find…words worth reading.

This book is lovingly dedicated to C. G. Meador, Sr., better known to the Meador family as "Pa." The family's "Stone of Ebenezer," Pa always had a spring in his step, a twinkle in his eye, and loved us just the way God had created us. Most of the stories in this book are centered around this wise and wonderful man who always took the time to be with a wide-eyed and inquisitive little girl.

I love you, Pa. "Choctaw"

Acknowledgments

I am forever grateful to have been a part of two loving and wonderful families. Although this book is about my father's side, the Meador family, I would be greatly in error if I did not thank my mother, Beth Meador and her family, the Steadman family. Throughout my life, each of these family members loved, guided, and encouraged me in all my endeavors. They made me the person I am today and gave me my love for food and family.

My three daughters, Elizabeth, Emily, and Erin are forever telling me to follow my dreams and have supported me in all my writings and adventures. They gave me recipes, tested my food, and everything in between.

I want to thank Indigo River Publishing for their support and development of this project. After praying one day for blessings on the Meador land, thirty minutes later I received a phone call from this energetic group wanting to tell the story of this beautiful log cabin and land in Hattiesburg, MS. Without them, these stories and menus would have never come together in book form. I especially want to thank Adam Tillinghast for his tireless efforts in making this project a part of himself, living and breathing life into each menu, memory, and picture with amazing creativity and talent.

Finally, I want to thank my husband, Eddie Smith. Without him, Meador Homestead would have remained a dilapidated, worn out house, and eventually been lost in time. His love and support in any endeavor in my life does not go unnoticed and appreciated. I love him very much.

Contents

Spring

Camellia Brunch 14
New Orleans Style

Dinner in the Dogtrot 22
A Supper at Sunset

Magnolias and Mother's Day 30
For a Special Mom

Sweet Sixteen Party 36
A Ms. Sippy Tea

Summer

A "RoyalTea" Celebration 46
A Bridal Wedding Tea

Lunch from the Land 54
A Vegetable and Fruit Dinner from the Garden

Dining "Alfresco" 60
Entertaining in the Open Air

Picnic by the Pond 68
A Picnic with Your Special One

A Millinery Luncheon 74
A Garden Luncheon with all the Accessories

Fall

Game Day Spread 82
A Tailgate Party to Kick Off the Season

Ladies Luncheon on the Lawn 90
A Southern Food Luncheon Tea

Dinner on the Boards 98
"Old South Style"

A Festival of Food 106
A Menu Honoring Famous Mississippians and Their Favorite Food

A Thiskamas Affair 114
A Holiday Harvest with New Traditions

Winter

A New Beginnings Luncheon Tea 126
  A Welcoming Tea for Any Occasion

A Circuit Rider's Tea 138
  A Soup and Sandwich Meal for Those on the Go

Fireside Candlelight Dinner 146
  A Romantic Evening for Two

Cast Iron Cooking 152
  Cabin Comfort Food

Christmas at the Cabin 162
  Comfort and Joy

Anytime Celebrations

Rise and Shine 172
  Bed and Breakfast Food

Poker Night with Price 180
  A Game Gathering Meal

Harvest of Memories 186
  A Come to Sunday Dinner Meal

A Friends Forever Luncheon 194
  Feasting with Friends

A Family Gathering 200
  Rekindling Ties with Lovin' Spoonfuls

Sewing Circle and Southern Sides 212
  A Luncheon with Special Friends

Index 218
Credit Recipes 220
Other Credits 221

Welcome to Meador Homestead

The Meador Homestead cabin is listed on the National Register of Historic Places and has been open to tourists and bed and breakfast guests since 2010.

Just off one of the busiest intersections, and well inside the city limits of Hattiesburg, MS, is a two room, dogtrot cabin nestled amidst hundred year old cedars and crepe myrtle trees. A small paved road leads you directly to this strongly built structure that seems to sit in splendid isolation, oblivious to the sounds of the busy highway, just a stone's throw away. It is a living museum of late nineteenth century architecture, built in 1884. Although it was a typical unassuming structure of its day, it proudly shows off its humble beginnings. The cabin is warm and inviting like the land that surrounds it, for it continues to emulate its appealing rustic feel. It had been a dairy farm after all, and therein lies the charm of Meador Homestead.

Even though the cabin expresses reverence for the past, its ongoing vitality and purpose still manage to be uncompromisingly of the present. There are glimpses of "life" everywhere: portraits of family members, past and present; books left opened to a favorite spot, games unfinished as if play has been interrupted by something much more enticing, and music records piled on top of each other, ready to be played and inviting a dance. Flowers freshly picked from the land tumble out of small vases, and sounds of laughter and gentle talk with friends over a cup of tea can be heard. And of course, coming from the kitchen and permeating throughout the air are the smells of southern cooking at its best.

Meador Homestead is a place of the past filled with memories of a family who lived their lives with hopes in their tomorrows and lots of love for each other. It is also a place of the present as guests are welcome to spend the night at its Bed and Breakfast and enjoy the true southern hospitality of Simply TeaVine, Mississippi's #1 tea room. The tea room serves southern delicacies and soothing loose leaf tea to visitors who want to destress and share in friendly conversation over a table laden with good food and drink.

That is what this book is all about—a way for you to experience over one hundred years in the life of a simple family, their way of living, and the food they loved to eat. The stories are told through my eyes as a granddaughter and my love for the family who lived on this hill. The food is what I grew up eating in the south, and the menus created tie history of the family with special times we have had and continue to have at Meador Homestead. Pictures in the book visually tie the stories and food together, inviting you to enjoy this tiny southern piece of heaven.

I have included a lot of food for each menu. What the family particularly liked and what was available in season usually defined the choice of food for each event. Please feel free to try as much or as little as you wish. This book is for you to enjoy those special times in life with family and friends. So, Y'all come on in. Eat, Drink, and Make Memories!

Dean Meador Smith

www.simplyteavine.com and
www.meadorhomestead.com

Ordering: 3304 Southaven Drive,
Hattiesburg, MS 39402
601-268-3236

"*For I am your guest, a traveler passing through, as my ancestors were before me.*"
Psalm 39:12

Spring

Camellia Brunch
NEW ORLEANS STYLE

Dinner in the Dogtrot
A SUPPER AT SUNSET

Magnolias and Mother's Day
FOR A SPECIAL MOM

Sweet Sixteen Party
A MS. SIPPY TEA

Camellia Brunch
New Orleans Style

MENU

Fruit in Orange Cup

French Market Doughnuts

Eggs Benedict

Grilled Asparagus

Grits Martini

Bananas Foster

Annie's Assam Tea or Café au Lait

Decorations: Use the Mardi Gras colors of purple, green, and gold. Gold doubloons, a variety of colored beads, and masks surrounded by camellias create the centerpiece for a festive party table.

Special Note: We use an Assam tea which is a bold, black tea from the Assam region of India. Grandmother Annie Dean Meador was a student at Mississippi Women's College in 1917, which later became William Carey University in honor of the English missionary who served for decades in India. Thus we call this coffee-like tea "Annie's Assam," the signature tea of the university in Hattiesburg. Add milk to make it extra delicious.

There is always so much abloom at historic Meador Homestead. The land's rich kaleidoscope of color welcomes guests year-round. Yet, the floral wonderland shines brightest and is most fragrant when the end of February comes and spring explodes with colors from the azaleas and camellias. It is a king's feast of colors and emits the feeling as if a festive Mardi Gras parade is passing by. Each spectator scrambles to catch a glimpse of the purple, pink, and white buds bursting forth from the green foliage like corks from a champagne bottle. It is therapy for the soul, and so it was for my grandfather when he lovingly placed each bush into the ground.

My grandmother Dean was the love of his life. She wasn't much of a cook, or so he said, but she loved good food and fun and knew how to get a recipe. New Orleans was their favorite place to visit—and to eat, and if she discovered a delectable dish that took her breath away, she would march right back into the kitchen of a Bourbon or Royal Street restaurant and charm her way into receiving the chef's secret recipe. With the ingredients scribbled down on a napkin or scrunched up piece of paper, she would return back to the homestead in Mississippi, and the tasty and delicious food would inevitably wind up on the Meador dinner table for all to enjoy.

Dean was also one of Hattiesburg's first women entrepreneurs. Borrowing $30 from the bank, she opened Meador Linen Supply Company, and during WWII, she serviced all the linens at Camp Shelby, the army base in Hattiesburg. She was bright, yet sweet, and I am proud to be her namesake. Her life was cut short, however, because of cancer. For a period of time, the light went out in my grandfather. To commemorate her love and medicine for his soul, he took on the project of planting camellias and azaleas all over the Meador Homestead land. Now each year in the spring, his unbashful love of his Dean is seen everywhere.

What could be more beautiful than this story and the land's brilliant palette as a backdrop for a New Orleans brunch with French classics? We start the party off with our French doughnuts. Café du Monde, a restaurant that my grandparents loved to visit, serves these mouthwatering and messy delicacies for thousands of visitors to the Big Easy. It has been one of our favorite family places to go after a good night's rest, a game at the Super Dome, or a late date stroll through the French Quarters. Next is our creamy cheese grits served in a martini glass to bring on a party feel to the table. The colors of Mardi Gras are seen in the orange cup with fruit and grilled asparagus. I especially like the Eggs Benedict recipe because the Blender Hollandaise Sauce is so easy to make and just as tasty as the sauce you cook over a stove. The Bananas Foster recipe comes from the old and famous Brennan's restaurant in New Orleans. This menu puts everyone in the mood to let the good times roll!

FRUIT IN ORANGE CUP

Various fruit with Mardi Gras colors: kiwi, oranges, cantaloupe, honeydew, peaches, purple grapes, for example.

Carve a cup out of a navel orange and fill with fruit of choice.

Previous page: Commemorative Camellia & Festive Fruit Cup
Right: Our next Master Chef
Below: Love blossoms at Meador Homestead (C.G. & Annie Dean Meador)

FRENCH MARKET DOUGHNUTS

1 cup milk

¼ cup sugar

¾ tsp salt

½ tsp nutmeg

1 pkg active dry or cake yeast

2 Tbsp lukewarm water

2 Tbsp salad oil

1 egg

3 ½ cups all-purpose flour

Confectioners' sugar

Scald milk and add sugar, salt, and nutmeg. Cool. Sprinkle yeast into warm water, stirring until yeast is dissolved. Add oil, egg, and yeast to milk mixture and blend with a spoon. Add flour gradually, beating well. Cover with wax paper and a towel, and let rise in warm place until double in size. Turn dough on to a well-floured surface and knead gently. Roll into 18 x 12 inch rectangle. Cut into 3 x 2 inch rectangles. Cover with towel and let rise ½ hour. Fry doughnuts in vegetable or canola oil until golden brown. Drain on paper towels. Drop doughnuts in brown paper bag, sprinkle with confectioners' sugar, and shake well until thoroughly coated. Serve hot. Yield: 36 doughnuts.

EGGS BENEDICT

4 eggs

4 buttered English muffins halves

4 slices ham, cut into 3-inch rounds

Blender Hollandaise Sauce (recipe below)

Fill a large, non-aluminum saucepan with 1½ inches water; bring to a boil. Reduce heat to simmer. (Do not allow water to boil.) Break eggs, one at a time, into a custard cup. Hold lip of cup near water; gently slip egg into water. Simmer until eggs reach desired degree of doneness. Remove eggs with a slotted spoon; drain well.

Place 1 slice of ham on each half of an English muffin. Top each with a poached egg and cover with Hollandaise sauce. Garnish with grilled asparagus on top or on the side. Serve immediately. Yield: 4 servings.

BLENDER HOLLANDAISE SAUCE

¼ cup butter or margarine

1 egg yolk

1 Tbsp lemon juice

¼ tsp salt

⅛ tsp hot sauce

Melt butter. Combine egg yolk, lemon juice, salt, and hot sauce in container of an electric blender; process until mixed, about 3 seconds. Turn blender to low; add butter to yolk mixture in a slow, steady stream. Turn blender on high and process until thick. Keep warm.

*The consumption of raw or undercooked eggs may increase your risk of food-borne illness, especially to children and the elderly.

Clockwise from right: *Family WWII memorabilia, Let the good times roll!, So delicious it should be illegal, A floral wonderland*

GRILLED ASPARAGUS

Fresh asparagus

Olive oil

Garlic salt

Lemon pepper

Cooking spray

Wash asparagus and trim bottoms of asparagus to the tender portion of asparagus. Place asparagus on a cooking sheet and drizzle with olive oil. Season with salt and pepper. Spray cooking spray on top of asparagus and grill or cook at 350 degrees for 20 to 30 minutes or until crisp-tender.

GRITS MARTINI

3 (10 oz) cans condensed chicken broth

½ cup whipping cream

1 cup uncooked quick-cooking grits

2 cups shredded sharp cheddar cheese

Garnish:
Colored toothpicks

Purple onion

Green olives

Cheddar cheese

Combine chicken broth and whipping cream in a large saucepan; bring to a boil. Stir in grits, and return to a boil. Cover, reduce heat, and simmer for 5 to 7 minutes. Stir in cheese and cool 10 minutes. Place grits in a martini glass and place colored toothpick kabob of green olive, slice of purple onion, and cube of cheese in grits as garnish.

Top: *Mardi Gras in a glass*
Middle & bottom: *Beautiful Azaleas and Camellias set the scene for a party brunch*

BANANAS FOSTER

4 Tbsp brown sugar

2 Tbsp butter

2 bananas, peeled and cut lengthwise

1 oz banana liqueur

2 oz white rum

Vanilla ice cream

Melt sugar and butter in a stainless steel or aluminum skillet. Add banana and sauté until tender. Pour in liqueur and rum and flame. Baste until flame dies. Pour over vanilla ice cream. Serve and eat immediately. Serves 2.

Around: Bananas Foster & bursts of spring - worth the trip to Meador Homestead

21

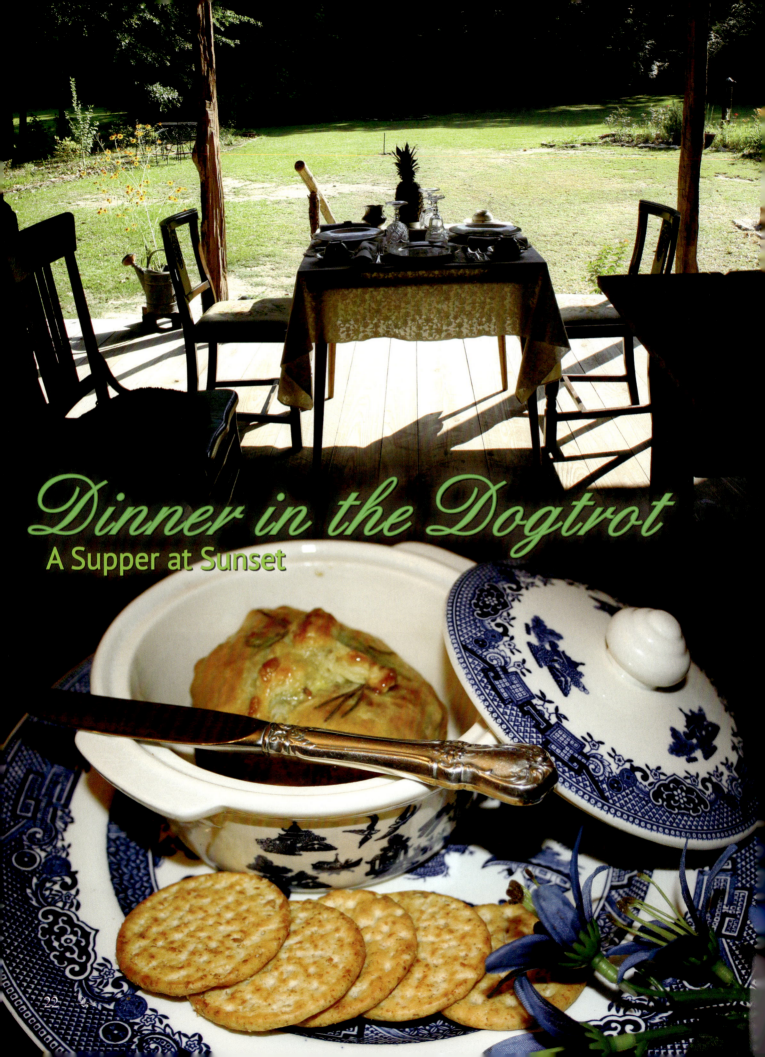

Dinner in the Dogtrot
A Supper at Sunset

MENU

Brie en Croute

Peach Tea Punch with Simple Sugar

Garden Salad with Russian Dressing

Boston Butt Pork Roast

Grandmother's Sweet Potato Casserole

French Bread • Squash Casserole

Strawberry Pie • Frosty Strawberry Squares

Decorations: Set up table in dogtrot or on a porch. Use heirloom china, linen, and small mementos from the family. We used the china, crystal, and silverware found in the cabin, dating back to the 1800s.

I never knew how important a dogtrot was to a cabin. It was in this open breezeway that most of the activities of the home took place in its earlier time. This long hallway was where domestic chores were done by the women and most of the meals were eaten, since it was the coolest place to get away from the hot temperatures of the South. One can sense the spirit of the family as they sat and churned for butter, shelled peas from the field, or spun at the loom.

As a child and young woman, I only knew it as the entrance hallway to the home. Long since had a front door been added and the ceiling lowered, with modern electricity replacing the candle and gas lights. The place still maintained its welcoming feel, however, for you knew when you entered, you were about to be with ones you loved dearly.

And it was still a place of activity. Bookshelves—or to me, treasure chests—lined the walls, waiting to be opened to the plethora of books collected by my grandfather, an avid reader. Later I discovered other family treasures of the past: an original deed signed by President Grover Cleveland, old love letters, tin pictures, and other memorabilia that opened up the story of who this family was, how they lived, and the values they stood for. Today, the dogtrot has been restored to its former glory and is still the center of activity as overnight guests and visitors continue to be welcomed with old-fashioned southern hospitality.

Builders knew how to place the cabin in a position so that a breeze would always run through it. At Meador Homestead, a constant current of air moves through the passageway where one can catch the welcome breeze. In the late summer, the air is full of hummingbirds, attracted by several hand-blown glass feeders. It gives the sense of one sitting in a peaceable kingdom. From every angle, the dogtrot offers a restful view, from the shaded flower garden of azaleas, camellias, and hydrangeas to the sprawling green open vista of a field with a multitude of daffodils and fruit trees blooming. It is above these trees that one takes in beautiful sunsets at suppertime.

The long, open passageway seems to invite a meal that would be both hearty and simple, one as satisfyingly direct as its setting. And oh, what a spot to dine! We set up a table there to enjoy the sunset and a scrumptious meal to be eaten in the approaching cool of the evening. Enjoy!

BRIE EN CROUTE

⅓ cup dried cherries, softened

½ pkg Pepperidge Farm puff pastry sheets (1 sheet)

1 egg

1 Tbsp water

Flour for rolling pastry

¼ cup chopped toasted pecans

¼ cup honey

½ tsp chopped fresh rosemary leaves

1 (13.2 oz) Brie cheese round

Pastry scraps and rosemary (opt)

Crackers of your choice

Apple wedges

Soften cherries in ½ cup hot water. Drain, pat dry, and set aside. Thaw pastry sheet at room temprature until easy to handle. Heat oven to 400 degrees. Beat egg and water in a small bowl and reserve. Unfold the pastry sheet on lightly floured surface. Roll sheet into a 14-inch square. Mix cherries, pecans, honey, and rosemary in bowl. Spread cherry mixture onto center of square. Top with cheese. Brush edges of pastry with egg mixture. Fold 2 opposite sides over cheese. Trim remaining 2 sides of square to 2 inches from edge of cheese. Fold sides up onto cheese and press edges to seal. Place seam-side down onto baking sheet. Decorate top with pastry scraps or additional rosemary, if desired. Brush with egg mixture. Bake for 20-25 minutes or until pastry is deep golden brown. Let stand for 45 minutes and serve with crackers and apples.

PEACH TEA PUNCH WITH SIMPLE SUGAR

4 cups water

3 family-size tea bags

2 cups fresh mint leaves

1 (33.8 oz) bottle peach nectar

½ (12 oz) can frozen lemonade concentrate, thawed

½ cup Simple Sugar Syrup (recipe below)

1 liter bottle ginger ale, chilled

1 liter bottle club soda, chilled

Fresh peaches for garnish (opt)

Bring 4 cups water to a boil; add tea bags and mint leaves. Boil 1 minute and remove from heat. Cover and steep for 10 minutes. Discard tea bags and mint. Pour into a gallon container and add peach nectar, lemonade, and simple sugar. Cover and chill overnight. Pour chilled tea mixture into a punch bowl. Stir in ginger ale and club soda, just before serving. Garnish with fresh peaches, if desired.

Simple Sugar Syrup:
2 cups sugar

1 cup water

Bring sugar and water to a boil. Continue to boil, stirring for 4 minutes or until sugar is dissolved and mixture is clear. Cool to room temperature. You can sweeten any iced tea with this syrup since it dissolves better in cold tea than sugar cubes or granulated sugar.

GARDEN SALAD WITH RUSSIAN DRESSING

Salad greens of your choice

Hard boiled eggs, sliced

Sliced tomatoes, or cherry tomatoes

Onions, sliced

Other vegetables of your choice

Make a green salad and garnish with boiled eggs, tomatoes, onions, and other vegetables of your choice. Serve dressing on the side.

Dressing:
1 pint mayonnaise

½ cup chili sauce

½ cup ketchup

1 cup pickle relish

2 hard cooked eggs, grated

4 green onions or 1 white onion, finely chopped

2 Tbsp finely chopped parsley (opt)

Mix all ingredients. Store covered in refrigerator. Keeps well.

25

BOSTON BUTT PORK ROAST

Below: Finger-lickin' Food
Facing page: Scenes from the Dogtrot, Family Casserole Dish (c. 1865), Brie Prep

8-10 lb pork shoulder roast

Spice mixture:

1 cup salt

¼ cup black pepper

Garlic powder

Rub spice mixture on meat and smoke in a smoker for 12-15 hours or until it falls apart. The temperature should be at 300-350 degrees and cooked until internal temperature of meat is at 160 degrees. Use oak wood for smoking.

GRANDMOTHER'S SWEET POTATO CASSEROLE

3 cups cooked sweet potatoes, mashed

1 cup sugar

2 eggs

1 tsp vanilla

½ cup sweet milk

⅓ cup butter

1 cup brown sugar

⅓ cup flour

¼ cup butter

Miniature marshmallows

1 cup chopped nuts

Combine sweet potatoes, sugar, eggs, vanilla, milk, and butter. Place in greased casserole. Combine brown sugar and flour. Sprinkle over sweet potato mixture. Cut bits of butter and place on top. Bake at 350 degrees for 30 minutes. Place marshmallows on top and cover with the chopped nuts and melt. Yield: 10 servings.

FRENCH BREAD

Purchase French bread from your local bakery.

SQUASH CASSEROLE

6 -8 yellow squash, sliced

½ stick margarine

2 small onions, chopped and divided

Salt and pepper to taste

1 bell pepper, diced

1 can cream of mushroom soup

American-style salad Crispins

Place squash, margarine, 1 onion, and salt and pepper in a 3-quart saucepan. Cover with water and cook slowly until squash is soft. Drain. In a casserole dish, alternate layer of cooked squash with layer of other chopped onion, bell pepper, and soup. Top with salad Crispins. Bake at 350 degrees for 30-45 minutes.

STRAWBERRY PIE

1 quart strawberries, divided

¾ cup sugar

2 Tbsp cornstarch

2 Tbsp lemon juice

1 (8 oz) pkg cream cheese, softened

2 Tbsp milk

2 Tbsp sugar

9-inch pastry shell, cooked

¼ cup red currant jelly, melted

Wash strawberries and remove greens, reserving half for the top. In saucepan, crush remaining berries and stir in sugar, cornstarch, and lemon juice. Cook over low heat, stirring constantly until thickened and clear; set aside to cool. In small bowl with mixer at medium speed, beat cheese until smooth. Blend in milk and 2 Tbsp sugar. Spread over bottom of pie shell. Spoon crushed strawberry filling over cheese. Cut reserved berries in half lengthwise and arrange on top. Lightly brush melted currant jelly over top for glaze.

FROSTY STRAWBERRY SQUARES

1 cup sifted flour

¼ cup brown sugar

½ cup chopped walnuts or pecans

½ cup butter, melted

2 egg whites

1 cup sugar

1 cup heavy cream, whipped

2 cups diced fresh strawberries or 1 (10 oz) pkg frozen stawberries, thawed

2 tsp lemon juice

Garnish with fresh strawberries

In small bowl, stir together first four ingredients. Spread evenly in shallow baking pan. Bake for 20 minutes in 350 degree oven, stirring occasionally. Sprinkle ⅔ of this crumbled mixture in a 13 x 9 x 2 inch baking pan. Allow to cool. Combine egg whites and sugar in a mixing bowl and beat at high speed until stiff peaks form. In a separate mixing bowl, whip heavy cream. Fold berries, lemon juice, and whipped cream into egg whites and sugar mixture. Spread over the crumbled mixture in the baking pan. Top with remaining crumb mixture. Freeze for 6 hours or overnight and cut into squares. Top with fresh strawberries. Yield: 15 squares 2 ½" x 3".

Both Pages: *The beautiful flowers at the Dogtrot, Our Families Faithful "Friend", Strawberries at their best.*

Magnolias and Mother's Day
For a Special Mom

MENU
Evelyn's Banana Punch
Grandmother's Apricot Congealed Salad
Dean's Twice-Baked Potatoes
Peggy's Squash Soufflé
Nancy's Green Beans with Catalina
Elizabeth's Biscuits
Mom's Easy Chicken
Andrea's Pineapple Cream Pie

Decorations: Magnolias bloom everywhere during May in the South. Use these to adorn your table, but cut your magnolias right before you decorate to avoid browning. A scented candle enhances the table and is a perfect gift. Add a card entitled "To the Original Steel Magnolia." It will be a day she will never forget!

"Ah, the sweetest perfume—magnolia blossoms blowing in the wind and a mother's skin"

What does love smell like?

In front of the cabin stands a huge magnolia tree. At least a hundred years old, it stands in line with the massive cedar trees where the old wagon trail from Gordonville (now Hattiesburg) to the north once was. No one knows who planted the tree. It could have been planted by the Choctaw Indians living on the land to find their footpath, or it could simply be a gift from God. But every year, it marks the beginning of May in Mississippi as its blossoms softly waft sweet fragrance in the breeze.

A mother is born at her baby's first breath. With each step of life, the mother grows in experience and wisdom. She becomes like a shade tree to her loved one, providing protection from the harshness of life. By her words and example, she leaves a mark, just like the magnolia tree, reminding her dear ones of the path they should go. A loving mother is planted by God and is one of His greatest gifts to mankind.

On May 14, 1914, President Woodrow Wilson officially proclaimed the national observance of Mother's Day to be held on the second Sunday of every May. I often wonder how that first Mother's Day was observed at the Meador cabin. When my great-grandfather married into the Arnold family, he brought his mother to live with his new wife and her mother. Two mother-in-laws, along with a new mother, had to share their china, furniture, and way of life in a two-room cabin. Oh, if walls could only talk! In the case of the cabin, they did, in the form of a letter written by my grandfather in 1917. From it, we see how these mothers and the women around him left their mark.

"I had the dearest mother on earth, as you know. I also have the dearest sister on earth, as you also know. Both of them have been and are far better than I shall ever be or have ever been. Pure and noble womanhood can command respect without force, can and must be respected by all men, no matter how low. Purity has protected more women than vice ever destroyed, although it sometimes seems hidden, and as long as there are women like mama, Clara, and Dean, the world need not fear."

People say I look like my mama and my daughter looks like me. The seventh generation granddaughter who visits the cabin looks like we all did when we were babies. Mothers leave a mark on who will come after them. And whether it is the smell of hands from picking magnolias on the land or in the case of my mother, cookies baking and recipes created in the kitchen, these mothers indelibly leave the fragrance of love.

Our menu comes from some special mothers who have been a shade tree of love and protection to their loved ones. As the aroma of cooking fills the kitchen, remember this is the smell of love. Enjoy!

EVELYN'S BANANA PUNCH

4 cups sugar

6 cups water

1 large can frozen lemonade

1 large can pineapple juice

2 large cans frozen orange juice

5 ripe bananas

9 (12 oz) cans lemon-lime soda

Dissolve sugar in water. Add lemonade, pineapple, and orange juices. Blend bananas well in a blender; add to juices and mix well. Put in 3 milk cartons and freeze. Take out of freezer 3 hours before serving. Add 3 cans soda to each carton. Be sure soda is cold but not frozen.

GRANDMOTHER'S APRICOT CONGEALED SALAD

1 (6 oz) pkg orange-flavored gelatin

1 cup hot water

1 cup apricot nectar

1 cup miniature marshmallows

2 large bananas, mashed

⅔ cup chopped pecans

2 Tbsp melted butter

1 egg, beaten

½ cup sugar

1 (8 oz) can crushed pineapple, undrained

2 Tbsp flour

1 (3 oz) pkg cream cheese, softened

1 cup whipping cream, whipped

Flaked coconut (opt)

Dissolve gelatin in hot water. Add apricot nectar, marshmallows, bananas, and nuts. Chill until slightly thickened. In a saucepan, combine butter, egg, sugar, pineapple, and flour. Cook over low heat, stirring constantly until thickened. Add cream cheese, stirring until melted; cool. Fold in whipped cream. Combine cooked mixture and gelatin mixture. Spoon into an 8 x 11 inch pan. Sprinkle with coconut if desired. Chill until firm and cut into squares. Serves 8.

Previous page: *A very special day*
Clockwise from above: *Cool refreshment, The original mothers of the cabin (1913), classic southern flavors from moms, Mother's Day, Mother & Baby (how sweet!), Hand stitched magnolia by Martha Ginn*

DEAN'S TWICE BAKED POTAOES

4 medium baking potatoes

1 cup sour cream

½ cup milk

½ stick butter, softened

Salt and pepper

1 ½ cup shredded cheddar cheese, divided

1 (3 oz) pkg real bacon bits, divided

2 green onions, finely chopped

Preheat oven to 350 degrees. Bake potatoes wrapped in foil for 1 hour. When cool, slice potatoes in half lengthwise and scoop out potato, leaving skin as a cup to fill. Combine potatoes, sour cream, milk, butter, salt, pepper, ¾ cup cheese, and half of bacon bits. Spoon mixture into shells and sprinkle with remaining bacon bits, cheese, and onions. Return to oven for 10 to 15 minutes until heated. Yield: 8 servings. If preparing in advanced, potatoes may be frozen before baked the second time.

PEGGY'S SQUASH SOUFFLÉ

2 cups cooked yellow squash

1 cup chopped onion

1 cup shredded cheddar cheese

1 cup evaporated milk

2 eggs

2 cups cracker crumbs, divided

¾ stick margarine

1 tsp salt

Pepper

Mix all ingredients together, saving part of crumbs for the top. Cook at 375 degrees for 40 minutes.

NANCY'S GREEN BEANS WITH CATALINA

Fresh or canned long green beans

Strips of bacon (opt)

Catalina dressing

Place beans on cookie sheet or baking dish. You can wrap a handful of beans with strip of bacon and secure with toothpick for appetizers. Pour dressing over beans and cook at 350 degrees for 20 minutes.

ELIZABETH'S BISCUITS

2 cups Bisquick mix

1 cup sour cream

1 stick butter, melted

Mix ingredients and drop by spoonfuls on cookie sheet. Bake at 375 degrees for 10 minutes. Yield: 10 biscuits

Clockwise from right: Mom & daughters, Pineapple over pie makes a sweet addition, Magnolia in the Magnolia State, Four generations, Mom reading us a story

MOM'S EASY CHICKEN

6 meaty chicken breasts

1 can tiny pearl onions

Salt and pepper

1 can cream of mushroom soup

⅛ cup sherry (opt)

¼ lb cheddar cheese, grated

Place chicken in baking dish. Add onions, and season with salt and pepper. Mix soup and sherry and pour over chicken. Grate or sprinkle cheese over top. Cover and place in a 350 degree oven for 45 minutes. Uncover and continue baking for a good 30 to 45 minutes more.

ANDREA'S PINEAPPLE CREAM PIE

2 graham cracker pie shells

1 large tub of Cool Whip

1 can condensed milk

1 small can crushed pineapple, well drained

2 lemons (juice only)

½ cup chopped pecans

Beat cool whip in mixer well. Then add condensed milk and beat. Add pineapple, lemon juice, and nuts. Pour mixture into pie crusts and chill 3 to 4 hours before serving. Recipe can be cut in half for 1 pie.

Sweet Sixteen Party
A Ms. Sippy Tea

MENU

Waldorf Sandwich • Chai Tea Mini Biscuits

White Chocolate Pretzels • Clotted Créme

Crabapple Jelly • Lemon Curd

$250 Cookie Recipe • Sweetheart Sugar Cookies

Carrot Cake Muffins • Cheese Delights

Slushy Punch • Cucumber Benedictine Sandwich

Coca Cola Cake • Basic Scones

It was May of 1971 when a host of teenage girls from the city came to the cabin for a party. Dressed in bell bottoms with bouffant hairstyles, we were graciously welcomed to gather on the screened-in front porch of the cabin to wait for everyone to arrive. While there, we were served cool, delicious punch from a crystal punchbowl. We took turns swinging in the porch swing before being herded through the dogtrot (then a hallway) and into the small wood-paneled den to play games and eat mouth-watering finger food.

Jessie, my step-grandmother, had prepared a graduation tea for me in celebration of the transition from a young girl in high school to the great open world of life and womanhood. She was the grandmother I knew as my own, and she felt the same way about me. I fondly remember going to the fish camp on the coast with her as a child and playing "Old Maid" and other card games. She took me to her childhood stomping grounds, Vicksburg, MS, to see many "Miss Mississippi" pageants and the great battlefield where my great-grandfather had served as a chaplain during the Civil War. Of course, I can't forget the many holiday meals she so lovingly prepared for our family at the cabin. My greatest memory, however, is this graduation party when she took the time to gather all my dear high school friends to share in a special time of my life. To me, she was the most giving and selfless person I knew. Although she was battling cancer at the time, she was determined to give me one last special memory with her, and nothing would steal her joy in doing this for me. I would graduate a few weeks later and indeed be off to college with a bright future ahead, but nothing would ever be able to erase that extraordinary graduation party at the cabin with special friends, special food, and a very special grandmother.

Our menu was created to celebrate those calendar moments in a young girl's life. It could be a graduation, a baptism, or a birthday as in this Sweet Sixteen celebration that was given for my first cousin's daughter, Savannah. We served our Ms Sippy tea, which is less food than a traditional afternoon tea, but it is enough for starving teenagers. The Slushy punch is the punch my mom has served for many graduation, birthday, and wedding parties.

My family has included two sandwiches as our savories, along with fruit and the traditional sweets. The food should be served on a three-tiered tray, giving the party the fanciness it deserves.

Also included in our menu is the Crabapple Jelly to be lathered on our Basic Scones. In years to come, our crabapples will come from the special tree planted for my granddaughter, Savannah Hagan, and back. She will be served this at her Sweet Sixteen party, surrounded by her friends a memory with her "Momma Dean" that will never go away!

Decorations: Have flower place card holders with treats as favors along with pictures of the honoree. Tea accoutrements for a ladies' traditional afternoon tea will make this party an unforgettable experience!

January 15, 1831

How dreadfully old I am getting! Sixteen! Well, I don't see as I can help it. There it is in the big Bible in father's own hand.

Katherine, born Jan. 15, 1815.

(Excerpt from *Stepping Heavenward* by Mrs. E. Prentiss)

WALDORF SANDWICH

1 (8 oz) pkg cream cheese

1 Tbsp mayonnaise

1 cup apple, peeled and chopped

1 Tbsp lemon juice

1 celery stalk, chopped

1 cup chopped pecans

2 Tbsp sugar

Small amount of crushed pineapple, drained

Raisin bread

One day before needed, coat apples with lemon and pineapple juices. Add remaining ingredients, except bread, and mix well. Cover and refrigerate. To serve, spread on raisin bread.

Previous page:** Savannah's Sweet Sixteen* ***Clockwise from left: *My 3 E's (Emily, Erin, and Elizabeth) Exceptional!, 1912 calendar girl, Crepe Myrtle at the cabin, Savories & sweets for a Sweet sixteen*

CHAI TEA MINI BISCUITS

1 cup 2% reduced-fat milk

3 regular-size chai tea bags

3 Tbsp granulated sugar

¼ tsp ground cinnamon

2 cups self-rising flour

Flour for kneading

¼ cup butter

½ cup powdered sugar

Heat milk in a saucepan for 2 to 3 minutes or until bubbles appear. Remove from heat. Add tea bags; cover and steep 5 minutes. Remove tea bags, squeezing excess into milk. Stir sugar, cinnamon, and flour together in a large bowl. Cut in butter with a pastry blender. Add ¾ cup milk mixture, stirring just until moistened. Turn dough out onto a lightly floured surface; knead gently with floured hands. Pat dough to ¾ inch thickness; cut with a cookie cutter. Place on a lightly-greased baking sheet. Bake at 400 degrees for 6 to 7 minutes or until golden. Let stand for 5 minutes. Whisk together 1 Tbsp reserved milk mixture and powdered sugar until smooth. Drizzle over warm biscuits. You can freeze these un-baked biscuits ahead of time without the glaze, adding glaze after cooking.

WHITE CHOCOLATE PRETZELS

1 (12 oz) pkg white chocolate almond bark

1 (9 oz) pkg small pretzels

Slowly melt almond bark in a pan or follow directions on package. Dip pretzels in white chocolate and lay on wax paper to firm. When firm, you may put in a covered bowl or in a bag.

CLOTTED CRÉME

Whipping cream

Powdered sugar

Almond extract

Whip cream. Blend in powdered sugar and almond extract to taste.

CRABAPPLE JELLY

4 cups crabapple juice

4 cups sugar

To prepare juice: Select firm, crisp crabapples, about ¼ underripe. Sort, wash, and remove stem and blossom ends; do not pare or core. Cut crabapples into small pieces. Add water, cover, and bring to boil on high heat. Reduce heat and simmer for 20 to 25 minutes, or until crabapples are soft. Extract juice by putting fruit in a damp jelly bag or fruit press.

To make jelly: Measure juice into kettle. Add sugar and stir well. Boil over high heat, or until mixture sheets on a spoon. Remove from heat; skim off foam quickly. Pour jelly immediately into hot containers and seal.

LEMON CURD

3 eggs

½ cup fresh or bottled lemon juice

1 cup sugar

1 stick butter, melted

Beat eggs in a glass bowl until fluffy. Stir in lemon juice, sugar, and melted butter. Microwave on high for 3 minutes. Remove and stir with a wire whisk. Repeat 3 times at 1 minute each. The mixture will thicken when it cools. Store in refrigerator up to two weeks.

$250 COOKIE RECIPE

2 cups butter

2 cups sugar

2 cups brown sugar

4 eggs

2 tsp vanilla

4 cups flour

5 cups blended oatmeal

1 tsp salt

2 tsp baking powder

2 tsp baking soda

1 (24 oz) pkg chocolate chips

1 (7-8 oz) Hershey bar, grated

3 cups chopped nuts

Cream butter and sugars. Add eggs and vanilla. In a separate bowl, mix flour, oatmeal (which has been measured and blended to a fine powder), salt, baking powder, and baking soda together and add to mixture of butter, sugars, eggs, and vanilla. Add chocolate chips, Hershey bar pieces, nuts, and mix. Roll into balls and place two inches apart on a cookie sheet. Bake for 10 minutes at 375 degrees. Yield: 112 small cookies or 56 large cookies.

SWEETHEART SUGAR COOKIES

1 cup butter, softened

1 cup sugar

1 tsp vanilla extract

1 large egg

2 ½ cups all-purpose flour

¼ tsp salt

Flour for rolling

2 tsp meringue powder

2 tsp water

Pink sanding or fine sugar

Preheat oven to 350 degrees. Beat butter, sugar, and vanilla with an electric mixer. Add egg, beating until blended. Combine flour and salt, and add it to butter mixture, mixing until blended. Divide dough into 2 equal portions; flatten each portion into a disk. Cover and chill 10 for minutes. Place 1 disk of dough on a heavily-floured surface and roll to 1/8 inch thickness. Cut with a heart shaped cutter. Place on lightly greased baking sheets. Repeat procedure for second disk of dough. Bake for 10 to 12 minutes or until edges are lightly browned. Let cool on baking sheet 5 minutes and then transfer to wire racks. Cool completely. Whisk together meringue powder and 2 Tbsp water. Brush cookies with mixture or dip cookies in mixture. Sprinkle with sanding sugar.

Clockwise from left: *Pear blossoms, Emily Anne's Crabapple tree, Flowers bring the beauty indoors.*

CARROT CAKE MUFFINS

1 ½ cups finely grated carrots

1 cup chopped nuts

1 small can crushed pineapple

2 cups sugar

4 eggs

1 ½ cup salad oil

2 tsp vanilla

1 Tbsp cinnamon

2 cups flour

2 tsp baking soda

Grease and flour 3 9-inch layer pans or muffin tins. Mix carrots, nuts, and pineapple; set aside. Mix sugar, eggs, salad oil, vanilla, cinnamon, flour, and baking soda; add carrot mixture. Pour into layer pans or muffin tins and bake for 10 to 30 minutes at 350 degrees. Allow muffins or cake to cool before icing.

Cream Cheese Icing:

1 (8 oz) pkg cream cheese

¼ lb butter

2 tsp vanilla

1 (1 lb) box powdered sugar

Blend cream cheese and butter. Add all other ingredients, mix well, and spread on muffins or cake.

CHEESE DELIGHTS

This recipe can be found on page 95.

CUCUMBER BENEDICTINE SANDWICH

1 cucumber, peeled and seeds removed

1 small onion, quartered

2 (8 oz) pkgs cream cheese, softened

3 Tbsp mayonnaise

2 tsp dried dill weed

½ tsp salt

Dash hot pepper sauce

Green food coloring (opt)

White bread

Parsley

Raw vegetables (opt)

Place cucumber in blender and pulse 5 times. Put in mixing bowl. Put onion in blender, pulse, and add to cucumber mixture. Combine cream cheese and next 4 ingredients; mix with cucumber. You can add food coloring, if desired. Cut bread with cookie cutter. Spread mayonnaise on bread and spread cheese mixture on one slice of bread. Top with remaining slice and garnish with parsley. For pretty presentation, put filling in cherry tomatoes, celery sticks, zucchini, or other vegetable of choice. Serves 20-40. Cucumber mixture freezes well.

Left: *Some girls go with any occasion*
Right: *Ah, to be young again!*

SLUSHY PUNCH

Amount of water in orange juice can

3 cups sugar

1 (46 oz) can pineapple juice

1 large can frozen orange juice

1 small can lemon juice

2 bottles ginger ale

Cherries

Mint

Lemon slices

Bring water and sugar to boil. Add pineapple, orange, and lemon juices, and mix. Freeze for 24 to 36 hours. Thaw until slushy. Chill ginger ale. When ready to serve, add bottles of ginger ale to the desired strength. Make a frozen mold of cherries, mint, and lemon slices to garnish punch in punch bowl.

COCA COLA CAKE

1 cup butter or margarine

1 cup coke

3 Tbsp cocoa

2 cups flour

2 cups sugar

½ cup buttermilk

1 tsp baking soda

2 eggs, well beaten

1 tsp vanilla

1 ½ cup miniature marshmallows

Mix butter, coke, and cocoa in saucepan and bring to a rapid boil. Pour over flour and sugar. Mix until blended. Add buttermilk, baking soda, eggs, and vanilla, mixing until smooth. Stir in marshmallows. Put into a well greased and floured sheet cake pan. Bake at 350 degrees for 30 minutes.

Frosting:

½ cup margarine

3 Tbsp cocoa

6 Tbsp coke

1 (1 lb) box powdered sugar

1 tsp vanilla

1 cup pecans

Bring ingredients to a boil margarine, cocoa, and coke. Take off heat and add sugar, nuts, and vanilla. Blend well and pour over cake.

BASIC SCONES

1 stick butter

½ cup sugar

3 cups self-rising flour

1 tsp cinnamon

¼ cup raisins

1 cup buttermilk

Flour for board

1 egg, beaten

Options to add to the scones:
Strawberries

Chocolate chips

Blueberries

Other fruit of your choice

Cut butter into sugar until it resembles cornmeal. Add flour, cinnamon, and raisins. Gently stir in buttermilk to form a soft dough. Turn out on a floured board and roll to desired thickness. Cut with biscuit cutters or as pie-shaped wedges. Place on greased baking sheet. Brush tops with beaten egg. Bake at 400 degrees, or 375 degrees in convection oven for 10 minutes. You can add strawberries, chocolate chips, blueberries, or other fruit for taste preference.

"March 21, 1971,
Our birthday dinner had been delayed a week for the simple reason 35 to 40 pretty little girl Seniors from Hattiesburg High School "took over" the place the previous Sunday for a party of their own. Their youthfulness and happiness evoked "nostalgic" memories for me to a time over 60 years ago when I too was a Senior and leaving Hattiesburg High."

C. G. Meador

Summer

A "RoyalTea" Celebration
A Bridal Wedding Tea

Lunch from the Land
A Vegetable and Fruit Dinner from the Garden

Dining "Alfresco"
Entertaining in the Open Air

Picnic by the Pond
A Picnic with Your Special One

A Millinery Luncheon
A Garden Luncheon with all the Accessories

A "RoyalTea" Celebration
A Bridal Wedding Tea

Menu

Savories: Smoked Salmon • Cottage Pie
Asparagus Chantilly • Mini Sausage Rolls
Cucumber Benedictine • Stuffed Strawberries with Crème
Cheese Delight Heart • Chicken Salad
Lavender and Honey Scones

Sweets: Petit Four Wedding Cakes
Wedding Cake Cookies
Westminster Abbey Chocolate Hat Cake
Miniature Cheesecakes • Peach Melba
Candies of the Heart • Scottish Shortbread Cookie

Teas to Be Served:
The King's Fancy (Scottish Breakfast Tea)
Blue Sapphire (a Kenyan black Tea)
Keemun Hoa Ya A (a Keemun estate tea from China)
Almond Cookie Green

Decorations: Adorn your table with the "Crown Jewels" or antique jewelry. Use bracelets as napkin rings, and decorate with pictures of the bride and groom. White lace and the finest china should be used.

Purchase your favorite heart-shaped candies and Scottish shortbread cookies.

My great-grandfather W. P. Meador was a preacher and a visionary. In 1904, he and a small group left the family's home church in downtown Hattiesburg, Main Street Methodist, and established a church in the most western part of the town on Red Street, later renamed Broad Street. My great-great-grandfather became the first preacher of the church with W.P. serving as a trustee and steward. It was there at Broad Street Methodist Church where he married Ms. Lena Arnold, the remaining daughter of the first family who lived in the cabin. The year was 1913 and with his mom and youngest boy, he settled into his new home at Meador Homestead. In front of the cabin was the only wagon trail and road connecting Hattiesburg to the north, and it was there where couples would hitch their horses or later come in their Model T's to get married.

My great-grandfather, wanting to make a special place for the bride and groom and their family, remodeled the north room by raising the ceiling to provide better "air conditioning." It was in this room where the bride and groom would sign their license and a reception would be held. The cabin is steeped in the history of making wedding days special days.

The "RoyalTea" Celebration was created to honor the marriage of Prince William of England and Kate Middleton. The menu, which is loaded with origins of British history, includes some of the favorite food of the Royal Family. There is always cause for celebration, however, when any wedding occurs, and an afternoon tea is a perfect way to honor someone on their special day. Guests will go away being glad they made the exclusive "invite list."

The menu consists of savories, scones, and sweets. A favorite savory of Prince William is Cottage Pie, or as most Americans say, "Shepherd's Pie." The term "cottage" pie was introduced in 1791 when the potato became an edible crop affordable for the poor, or "cottage" dwellers of England.

The second course of our wedding celebration is the serving of scones. The scone is said to have taken its name from a stone used at a coronation site for Scottish kings. The Stone of Scone, or Scone of Destiny, was taken to England by Edward I (my twentieth great-grandfather), in 1296 and kept in Westminster Abbey beneath the chair used during the crowning of British monarchs. The Stone of Scone was returned to Scotland in November 1996. We have used our own clotted crème in place of the Devonshire Crème of Devon, England. Lemon curd, honey, strawberries, or blueberries and crème are served as a complement to the scones.

The tea is finally topped off with the serving of the sweets. We created the Westminster Abbey Chocolate Cake in the form of a hat to compliment the fashionry of the guests attending the celebration. Peach Melba, the favorite of Prince Charles, was invented in 1892 to honor the Australian soprano, Dame Nellie Melba. Nellie Melba was performing in Wagner's opera *Lohengrin* at Covent Garden in London, England. The traditional bridal processional song comes from this famous opera. The wedding cake cookie is made by placing three different-sized sugar cookies on top of each other and decorating with frosting. The cookie is decorated by placing jewelry or fruit cake on the top, a tradition of English wedding cakes.

A bridal shower or reception is one of the most special days in a woman's life, and this regal tea is fit for a Queen!

SMOKED SALMON

½ cup smoked salmon pieces

½ cup cream cheese, softened

1 Tbsp lemon juice

1 Tbsp chopped dill

1 Tbsp heavy cream

Salt and pepper

2 slices wheat bread

Capers

Combine salmon, cream cheese, lemon juice, dill, and heavy cream in a food processor. Season with salt and pepper. Cut each slice of bread into 4 triangles. Spread with salmon mixture and garnish with tiny capers.

Previous page: The celebration begins
Above: Every wedding is a royal one
Above right: Cottage Pie - Prince William's favorite
Below right: Ladies in waiting for "RoyalTea"

COTTAGE PIE

1 lb ground chuck

1 onion, diced

3 carrots diced or package of mixed vegetables

2 Tbsp flour

1 Tbsp Italian seasoning

1 tsp Worcestershire sauce

2 Tbsp chopped fresh parsley

1 ¼ cups beef broth

¼ cup Burgundy wine

1 Tbsp tomato paste

Salt and pepper

4 potatoes, peeled and diced

¼ cup butter

1 cup milk

¼ lb shredded cheddar cheese

Preheat oven to 400 degrees. To make meat filling, brown beef then add onion and carrot or vegetable mixture and sauté until tender. Mix in flour, seasoning, Worcestershire sauce, and parsley. Stir in wine broth, tomato paste, salt, and pepper. Simmer mixture for 15 minutes until almost all of liquid has been absorbed. Spoon mixture into a 9-inch pie plate. Make Potato Topping: Boil potatoes until tender. Drain. Mash potatoes, adding butter and milk. Add salt and pepper to taste. Spread potatoes over beef filling. Sprinkle with shredded cheddar cheese. Bake in oven for 25 minutes, until top is browned and cheese is bubbly. Serve in mini pie tarts or small bowls.

ASPARAGUS CHANTILLY

Asparagus

1 cup mayonnaise

Lemon juice

Heavy whipping cream

Simmer asparagus until tender. In a bowl, mix mayonnaise with lemon juice and a couple Tbsp of heavy whipping cream. Serve asparagus cold with mayonnaise mixture in shooter glasses and garnish with a stem of asparagus.

MINI SAUSAGE ROLLS

Pillsbury crescent rolls

Small pkg cocktail wieners

Separate triangles of crescent rolls. Cut each triangle into two parts, making mini rolls. Place sausage on crust and roll. Bake at 350 degrees until brown.

CUCUMBER BENEDICTINE SANDWICH

This recipe can be found on page 42.

CLOTTED CRÈME

This recipe can be found on page 39.

CHEESE DELIGHTS

This recipe can be found on page 93.

STUFFED STRAWBERRIES WITH CRÉME

Large strawberries

Clotted Créme

Cut green from strawberry with knife to level where strawberry can stand upright. From top with knife, make 4 slits to open strawberry for filling. With cake decorator bag, fill strawberry with clotted créme.

LEMON CURD

This recipe can be found on page 39.

Right: *Scones and strawberries - fit for "RoyalTea"*
Far right: *Miniature wedding cakes - how sweet!*

Left: The savories of "RoyalTea"
Below: Family wedding cake topper

CHICKEN SALAD

This recipe can be found on page 93.

LAVENDER AND HONEY SCONES

1 stick butter

½ cup sugar

3 cups self-rising flour

1 tsp lavender

1 cup buttermilk

Flour for board

Milk and lavender for top of scones

Serve with:
Honey

Lemon curd

Devonshire or clotted crème

Blueberry preserves

Cut butter into sugar until it resembles cornmeal. Add flour and lavender; stir in buttermilk. Form a soft dough. Turn out on a floured board and roll to desired thickness. Cut with biscuit cutters or cut as pie-shaped wedges. Place on greased baking sheet. Brush tops with milk and sprinkle lavender on top. Bake at 375 degrees for 10 minutes in convection oven. Serve with honey, Devonshire or clotted crème, lemon curd and blueberry preserves.

PETIT FOUR WEDDING CAKES

1 (18.25 oz) pkg white cake mix

¼ tsp almond extract

Preheat oven to 350 degrees.

Prepare mix according to package directions and add almond extract.

Pour mix in an 11 x 13 pan and cook as on cake mix package. After cooling, cut into bite-size squares. Decorate with Fondant Icing.

Fondant Icing:
7/8 cup skim milk

3 Tbsp shortening

⅛ tsp salt

1 ½ tsp clear vanilla

1 ½ tsp butter flavoring

⅛ tsp almond extract

1 (2 lb) bag powdered sugar

In a microwave, combine milk, shortening, and salt. Remove from heat. Never return to heat; thin with hot milk. Add vanilla, butter flavoring, and almond extract. Add in sugar with mixer. Place rack of cake over wax paper to catch drips. Pour ½ cup icing over each cake. Cool on rack. When set, store in container. Yield: 5 cups.

Optional: To make a three-tiered wedding-style cake, pour batter two-thirds full into 2-inch 5-inch, and 8-inch cake pans that have been greased with cooking oil. Bake for 10 to 30 minutes depending on size of pan. Cool in pans and then on a wired rack. Frost with buttercream icing or frosting of choice.

WEDDING CAKE COOKIES WITH FROSTING

Sugar cookies or cookies
  of varying sizes

Decorator Icing

Fruit cake (opt)

Pick three cookies of varying sizes and place on top of each other. Fill between with decorator icing. The cookies can be decorated by placing fruit cake on its top, a tradition of many English wedding cakes. I adorned mine with some antique gold cuff links with two circles and a pearl, symbolizing the two wedding rings intertwined.

Basic Decorator Icing

1 ¼ cup Crisco

⅛ tsp salt

2 tsp clear vanilla

½ tsp butter flavoring

1 tsp powdered egg white

2 lbs powdered sugar

3-14 Tbsp hot milk, almost boiling

Food coloring

Blend the first 5 ingredients for icing and then add the sugar and hot milk. Use foods coloring with icing in small bowls for the various colors you want.

Above: A millinery's delight - our delicious hat cake
Left: The steps of Meador cabin - the altar of newlyweds!

WESTMINSTER ABBEY CHOCOLATE HAT CAKE

¾ cup shortening

2 ½ cups sugar

5 eggs

1 cup buttermilk

1 tsp baking soda

2 ½ cups flour

½ tsp salt

1 tsp vanilla

5 Tbsp cocoa

Boiling water

Chocolate frosting

Decorations for cake

Cream shortening and sugar together, adding sugar ½ cup at a time. Add well-beaten eggs. If using electric mixer, eggs may be added, unbeaten, one at a time. Beat well after each addition. Stir baking soda into buttermilk and add alternately with flour, about ¼ of each at a time. Add salt and vanilla flavoring. Dissolve cocoa in enough boiling water to make a smooth paste and add to batter. Bake in three greased, 8-inch layer cake pans or different sized pans to determine the shape of your hat. Cook in 300 degree oven for about 50 minutes. Test for doneness with a toothpick. Cool and ice with chocolate frosting and decorate your hat any way you want.

MINIATURE CHEESECAKES

Butter

10 graham crackers, crushed

1 (8 oz) pkg cream cheese, softened

¾ cup sugar

3 eggs, separated

1 (8 oz) carton sour cream

2 ½ Tbsp sugar

1 tsp vanilla

Toppings:
Strawberry pieces

Grape halves

Blueberry pie filling

Cherry pie filling

Butter the sides and bottoms of all 48 sections in 4 miniature muffin tins. Sprinkle with graham cracker crumbs and shake to coat. Beat the cream cheese and sugar together. Add egg yolks one at a time beating well. Beat the egg whites until very stiff and fold into cream mixture. Spoon filling into muffin tins almost to the top and bake in upper third of preheated 350 degree oven for 12 to 15 minutes. Remove from oven and cool. Cakes will sink in the middle. Mix together the sour cream, sugar, and vanilla. Drop about 1 tsp sour cream mixture in the center of each little cake. Bake 4 minutes in 400 degree oven. Cool before removing from pans. To facilitate removal from pan, loosen sides with a sharp knife, hold pan perpendicular to countertop, and ease out each tart with knife. Top each with a piece of fresh strawberry, a grape half, or a drop of blueberry or cherry pie filling. Freezes well. Yields 48 miniature cakes.

PEACH MELBA

For Peaches:
3 cups water

3 ½ cups sugar

1 tsp vanilla

2 Tbsp lemon juice

8 peaches

For Raspberry Sauce:
3 cups raspberries

¼ cup powdered sugar

1 Tbsp lemon juice

To Serve:
Vanilla ice cream

Whipped cream

Pecans

Put the water, sugar, vanilla, and lemon juice into a saucepan and heat to dissolve the sugar. Bring to a boil and bubble for 5 minutes. Cut the peaches in half and poach the halves in the sugar syrup for about 2 minutes. Test to see if the peaches are soft and remove to a plate. When all the peaches are poached, peel off skins and cool. To make the raspberry sauce, blend the raspberries, powdered sugar, and lemon juice in a blender. To assemble the Peach Melba, place a peach half on a plate or bowl beside a scoop of ice cream. Spoon the raspberry sauce over each and add a spot of whipped cream with pecans.

Left: The sweets of "RoyalTea" with the crown jewels

Lunch from the Land

A Vegetable and Fruit Dinner from the Garden

Decorations: Make your country table a rustic, casual feeling like a picnic. Use the bright colors of the garden with wildflowers, colorful zinnias, or sunflowers in dairy bottles. Baskets of fruit and vegetables become the centerpiece of this down-home meal. Fun and colorful paper products can be used over a red and white checkered tablecloth. Relax and enjoy!

MENU
Brussels Sprouts
Tomato Pie · Corn on the Cob
Fried Squash · Zucchini Bread
Blackberry Cobbler
Blackberry Sweet Tea

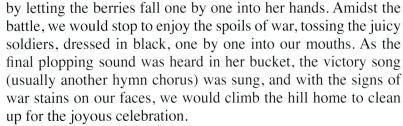

As a child, I was a serious soldier. Oblivious to any dangers ahead, I followed behind my leader, Ms. Lena. Through the wildflower field, around the cows grazing, and just down the hill, we would spot the enemy-held territory—the fearless blackberry patch by the pond. The war call was sounded (usually an Amazing Grace chorus), and we descended upon the intimidating company. Armed with an aluminum pie pan and spoon, I fearlessly banged away on my handmade weapon to scare the snakes away. Without flinching, and with calm resolution, my great-grandmother, wearing long sleeves, hat, and gloves, meticulously picked apart the thorny, warlike branches by letting the berries fall one by one into her hands. Amidst the battle, we would stop to enjoy the spoils of war, tossing the juicy soldiers, dressed in black, one by one into our mouths. As the final plopping sound was heard in her bucket, the victory song (usually another hymn chorus) was sung, and with the signs of war stains on our faces, we would climb the hill home to clean up for the joyous celebration.

The best part of picking blackberries on the land was the party. We all lived on the Meador Homestead hill, so I didn't have to travel far to get to my great-grandmother's home. I would enter to the smell of coffee brewing, and she would immediately proceed to pour me my coffee, which was only ¼ of a cup and the rest sugar and cream. Set for a queen, she showed me to my place at the table, and with fork in hand, my great-grandfather, Ms. Lena, and I would dive into the best blackberry cobbler ever. I will never forget those feasts of victory.

I have other fond food memories from the land. My grandfather had his own little garden under the huge pecan tree at the cabin that he said was just mine and his. He would help me plant my special row of watermelon seeds, and at the end of the season, we would devour with the ripe melons as if another battle had been won. The Meador family always had a huge garden on the hill, where the apple and peach trees are planted now, and we couldn't wait to lap up the bounty of vegetables and fruit grown from the land. The seeds had been planted and the battle won, thanks to hard work, the Lord, and the rich earth of the Meador Homestead land.

Our menu can consist of fresh vegetables and fruit grown in any garden. Everyone likes to celebrate with a vegetable meal from their victory garden, especially in the summer when everything has just been freshly picked. We chose to have Brussels sprouts, Fried Squash, Corn on the Cob, and Tomato Pie with juicy,

red tomatoes. The delicious Zucchini bread is made from the zucchini squash in the garden. If you have never had Zucchini bread, it tastes like Pumpkin bread. A cup of tea and a toasted slice of this bread put you in heaven! Finally, we have to end with my grandmother's famous Blackberry cobbler.

Today, I am making memories with my grandchildren. We now have thornless blackberry bushes, so my granddaughters can pick them, too, when they're not hitting their pie pans. We wear our boots and long sleeved shirts, still sing songs, and always celebrate the victory with good food and merriment.

TOMATO PIE

9-inch deep-dish pie crust

2 Tbsp unsalted butter

1 Tbsp extra virgin olive oil

1 medium onion, thinly sliced

2 tsp sugar

3 cloves garlic, thinly sliced

2-4 tomatoes, sliced into ¼ inch slices

4 oz cream cheese, softened

½ cup mayonnaise

2 Tbsp heavy cream

1 Tbsp sour cream

1 Tbsp champagne mustard

1 cup shredded Parmesan cheese

4 green onions, cut into pieces

½ tsp salt

½ tsp pepper

½ cup basil, torn

2 cups Swiss cheese

BRUSSELS SPROUTS

½ to 1 lb Brussels sprouts

Olive oil or butter

Garlic salt and lemon pepper

Italian Wishbone dressing

Bring a pot of water to full boil. Add Brussels sprouts and olive oil or butter. Cover and cook on low for 10 minutes. Drain sprouts and add seasonings with butter or Italian dressing.

Preheat oven to 400 degrees. Prick bottom of thawed crust with a fork. Bake crust for 10 minutes or until lightly browned. Remove from oven and cool. In a cast iron skillet, heat butter and olive oil over medium heat until it begins to sizzle. Add onions and sugar. Sauté until onions are caramelized. Add garlic and cook for 1 to 2 minutes. Remove onion and garlic from skillet and set aside to cool. Slice tomatoes. I use 2 big tomatoes or 4 small tomatoes.

In a food processor, combine cream cheese, mayonnaise, cream, sour cream, mustard, Parmesan cheese, and green onions. Mix well and set aside. In the cooled pie crust, layer half of the onions, cream cheese mixture, sliced tomatoes, salt, pepper, basil, and cheeses. Repeat layering using remaining ingredients.

Bake 35 minutes or until pie is bubbling and top is browned. Remove from oven and cool for 15 to 20 minutes before slicing.

CORN ON THE COB

This recipe can be found on page 206.

FRIED SQUASH

3 to 4 yellow squash, sliced

Salt and pepper

Cornmeal

Canola oil

Wash squash and cut up. Lay on dish and salt, so squash will adhere to cornmeal. Heat up oil in iron skillet. Roll squash in cornmeal and fry. Remove from heat and season with salt and pepper.

Previous page: *Bountiful harvest from the land*
Clockwise from below: *Capturing the colors inside a tomato pie, Innocent indulgence, Ripe for the picking, Off to Battle, The Meador army working the land, wildflowers in the Meador meadow*

BLACKBERRY COBBLER

1 cup sugar

1 Tbsp flour

⅛ tsp salt

3 cups blackberries

2, 9-inch deep-dish pie crusts

1 Tbsp butter

1 Tbsp lemon juice for other kinds of berries

Blend sugar, flour, and salt. Pour over 3 cups berries and stir until well coated. Pour into unbaked crust. Dot 1 Tbsp butter on top. Put on top crust and bake for 15 minutes at 450 degrees. Then reduce oven to 350 degrees and bake for 20 minutes.
Note: Other berries may be substituted. If using another type of berry, add 1 Tbsp lemon juice.

Clockwise from right: *Working bonnet, Lunch from the Land, Blackberry Cobbler, The spoils of victory, A sweetheart's sunflower, Blueberry bushes run wild at Meador homestead, Essential armor for a blackberry soldier*

ZUCCHINI BREAD

3 cups all-purpose flour

1 tsp salt

1 tsp baking powder

1 tsp baking soda

1 Tbsp ground cinnamon

3 eggs

1 cup vegetable oil

1 Tbsp vanilla extract

2 ¼ cups white sugar

2 cups grated zucchini

1 cup chopped walnuts

Grease and flour two 8 x 4 pans or four smaller loaf pans. Preheat oven to 350 degrees. Sift flour, salt, baking powder, baking soda, and cinnamon together in a mixing bowl. Beat in eggs, oil, vanilla, and sugar until well combined. Stir in zucchini and nuts that have been finely chopped. Pour batter into prepared pans. Bake for 40 to 60 minutes, or until fork inserted into center comes out clean. Cool in pan for 20 minutes. Remove bread from pan and completely cool.

BLACKBERRY SWEET TEA

2 cups fresh blackberries, or frozen blackberries, thawed

1 cup sugar

1 Tbsp chopped fresh mint

Pinch of baking soda

4 cups boiling water

2 family-size tea bags

2 ½ cups cold water

Whole berries (opt)

Combine blackberries and sugar in a container, and crush with a wooden spoon. Stir in mint and baking soda. Pour boiling water over tea bags; cover and steep 5 minutes. Discard tea bags. Pour tea over blackberry mixture and let stand at room temperature for 1 hour. Pour tea through a strainer, discarding solids. Stir in cold water. Cover and chill. Garnish with whole blackberries, if desired.

DINING "AL FRESCO"

Entertaining in the Open Air

MENU

Lemon Blueberry Sweet Tea

Figs Wrapped in Prosciutto

Minestrone Soup

Panzanella Salad with Cornbread Croutons

Meat Lasagna

Eggplant Zucchini Parmigiana

Fried Green Beans

Italian Breadsticks

Beehives

Strawberries and Balsamic Vinegar

Decorations: Since this meal is designed to be served out in the fresh air, make everything casual, simple, and comfy. An old door used as the tabletop over sawhorses with ladder-back chairs enhances the rustic and simple setting, but even serving the meal on a picnic table will make this meal just as pleasant and unforgettable for your outdoor entertaining. If possible, use sunflowers and Italian accoutrements to complete the view for a magnificent countryside meal.

My grandfather's love for the land of Meador Homestead was even greater than his love for the cabin. Where the house was the woman's domain, "Pa" was king of the countryside—planting huge gardens, growing beautiful flowers, feeding his flock of catfish in the pond, or just meandering down the cattle-created paths through the fields. My favorite times with him were walking through the woods and his pointing out to me the special places for him in his life: the sugar cane field, the chicken house, and the old spring where they drew water from, amongst many others. When writing home to his family in 1918 during World War I, he wrote from Washington DC: "I am hoping to get out by springtime so I can go to Mississippi and listen to the birds and fish. (You know fish call me in the spring just like they were human, or like I was a fish)." There was no way around it. He loved being outside at Meador Homestead.

I was in college when I made my first trip to Italy. My grandfather said, "I don't know why you want to go way over there when you have heaven right here." He was probably right, for when I am overwhelmed by an "alfresco" or "being in the open air" moment in Italy, my mind wanders back to Mississippi and the tiny beautiful hill I grew up on. At any given time, just like in Italy, I can see deer eating pears off the old pear tree in the yard, turkey slowly making their way to their supper of corn, or rabbits playfully engaged in a game of hide and seek with each other. Words cannot describe how I feel, only that I agree with him in saying indeed, "This is a little piece of heaven."

And so, we bring you to an "outdoor" table to enjoy the beautiful palette of the world God has created. We marry the two places we love the most: Italy and the cabin. Lemon Blueberry tea made with blueberries from the land and Figs Wrapped in Prosciutto or bacon for the antipasto is the perfect start to this outdoor event. There are thousands of variations for Minestrone soup because there are thousands of Italian grandmas. Like these grandmas, we thicken the soup and throw in the leftovers from the garden. Today you can add your own ingredients, simply cleaning out the refrigerator. Heaven should be so good with our next course of Panzanella salad and Cornbread croutons. The Lasagna entrée is a recipe given to me by my college roommate before my first trip to Italy. Just as delicious is our meatless eggplant and zucchini dish for vegetarians. We complete this course with green beans and Italian breadsticks, a true Italian classic fare. Guests will love the serving of "Beehives," a dolce dessert of fresh peaches wrapped in pie crust and served with a hard sauce. Our alfresco meal ends with fresh strawberries served in balsamic vinegar. How can you get more Italian than that?

As I sit in the "open air", I look back with fondness on the wonderful walks I had with my grandfather at the homestead. I recall the poem I gave him many years ago:

"If I should go before you….Into that other land….Just walk the woods in Autumn….and I will take your hand. Drink in all the beauty….that we have seen before….and know that I am with you…. as in the days of yore. Do not lament my passing….whenever I am gone…. Recall instead the joy of life…and pleasures we have known. The gentle winds that murmur low…will whisper that I care….then walk the woods in Autumn….and know that I am there."

by Glen Smith (a poem I gave to my grandfather in 1975)

Previous page: *Sunset at Meador Homestead*

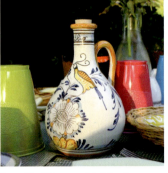

Clockwise from above: *Italian olive oil cariffe, Dinner with friends (il cena con amici), Breadstick heaven, Open air dining, Figs in Tuscany (Molto Bene!), An Italian Picnic (at Lake Como)*

PANZANELLA SALAD WITH CORNBREAD CROUTONS

Iron Skillet Cornbread, cooled completely

1 yellow bell pepper, diced

1 small red onion, diced

½ cup olive oil, divided

2 tsp lemon zest

¼ cup fresh lemon juice

½ tsp honey

Salt and pepper to taste

1 pt grape or cherry tomatoes, halved

½ cucumber, quartered and sliced

½ cup pitted and halved kalamata olives

½ cup fresh basil leaves, torn

Bake cornbread according to recipe on page 100. Cut cornbread into 1 inch cubes for croutons and bake in 400 degree oven to brown edges. Sauté bell pepper and onion in 1 Tbsp. olive oil, reserving 7 Tbsp of oil for dressing. Cook in a skillet for 5 minutes or until crisp and tender. Whisk together lemon zest, lemon juice, honey, and 7 Tbsp of oil. Salt and pepper to taste. Stir in onion mixture, tomatoes, and next 3 ingredients. Add toasted cornbread cubes and toss to coat. Serve immediately.

FIGS WRAPPED IN PROSCIUTTO

Fresh figs

Prosciutto or bacon

Cantaloupe, apples, or pears (opt)

Thinly slice prosciutto or bacon and wrap around figs. Secure with a toothpick. Bake figs in preheated oven of 350 degrees for 10 minutes. You can do this with any of the fruit.

LEMON BLUEBERRY SWEET TEA

1 (12 oz) package frozen blueberries or 2 cups fresh blueberries

½ cup lemon juice

3 family-size tea bags

¾ cup sugar

Blueberries and lemon (opt)

Bring blueberries and lemon juice to a boil. Cook, stirring occasionally, for 5 minutes. Remove from heat and pour through a strainer into a bowl, using back of a spoon to squeeze out juice. Discard solids. Bring 4 cups water to a boil in a saucepan. Add tea bags, and let stand 5 minutes. Discard tea bags. Stir in sugar and blueberry mixture, and add 2 cups cold water. Pour into a pitcher, and chill for 1 hour. Serve over ice and garnish with blueberries and lemon, if desired.

ITALIAN BREADSTICKS

2 cups sifted flour, divided

1 tsp dry yeast dissolved in 3 Tbsp warm water

3 Tbsp melted butter

1 tsp sugar

1 tsp salt

¼ cup lukewarm milk

Sesame seeds

Place 1 cup flour in mixing bowl. Blend in yeast mixture. Knead until smooth. Put in floured bowl and cover with a damp cloth. Leave in a warm place until double in bulk. Mix rest of flour, butter, sugar, and salt into a paste-like ball. Place on a floured board, add risen dough, and knead until smooth. Put dough into a large floured bowl, cover, and let rise to double in bulk. Turn and knead. Divide into 24 parts. Shape each into a rope six to seven inches long by rolling between hands. Place on buttered baking sheet one inch apart. Brush with milk and sprinkle with sesame seeds. Bake in 425 degree oven for 6 to 7 minutes.

MEAT LASAGNA

1 Tbsp butter

1 lb ground chuck

2 cloves garlic, chopped

1 (6 oz) can tomato paste

2 ½ cup canned tomatoes

1 tsp salt

½ tsp oregano

¾ tsp pepper

1 (8 oz) pkg wide lasagna noodles

1 ½ cup Swiss cheese, cut up

1 (12 oz) carton cottage cheese

Parmesan cheese, grated

Brown meat and chopped garlic in hot fat. Add tomato paste, canned tomatoes, salt, oregano, and pepper. Simmer 20 minutes. Cook wide noodles according to directions on package. In an oblong baking dish (3 qt) alternate layers of cooked noodles, Swiss cheese, cottage cheese, and meat sauce. Bake in a 350 degree oven for 20 to 30 minutes. Serve with grated Parmesan cheese.

STRAWBERRIES AND BALSAMIC VINEGAR

1 pint ripe strawberries (or fresh fruit of choice)

1 Tbsp sugar (or more to taste)

2 Tbsp balsamic vinegar

Hull the strawberries and cut them in half lengthwise. Place in a bowl and carefully toss with the sugar and vinegar. Toss just before serving and offer them in fancy glasses.

MINESTRONE SOUP

1 cup dried cannellini beans

8 cups chicken broth, divided

¼ lb pancetta or bacon, sliced and chopped

1 cup chopped onion

4 celery stalks, chopped

2 cups chopped carrots

2 Tbsp fresh parsley

2 garlic cloves, minced

1 Tbsp olive oil

2 cups canned kidney beans

2 cups canned tomato with juice

2 cups frozen green beans

2 cups garbanzo beans

1 Tbsp red wine

1 Tbsp basil

1 Tbsp oregano

1 cup kale or spinach, chopped

Salt, pepper, grated Parmesan cheese

Extra virgin olive oil

Cover cannellini beans with water and soak overnight. Drain the cannellini beans and place in a soup pot along with 3 cups of the chicken broth. Bring to a boil, cover, and simmer 1 hour until beans are tender. Strain the liquid, reserving liquid. Puree beans in a blender. Fry and brown the pancetta or bacon. Put in pot with pureed beans. Add olive oil to frying pan and add onion, celery, carrots, parsley, and garlic. Saute until tender and then add to the soup pot. Add the kidney beans, tomatoes, and other ingredients except for salt, pepper, and cheese; simmer for 1 hour. Add salt and pepper to taste and garnish with grated cheese and extra virgin olive oil. This soup tastes best made the day before. It also freezes well. Yield: 8 servings.

Left: *The lovely foods of Italy (Meravigliosa)*
Below: *Ed Meador (WWI veteran) brings home his Italian "Cup of Sacrifice",*

EGGPLANT ZUCCHINI PARMIGIANA

1 eggplant, peeled, cut into 12 ¼-inch slices

1 Tbsp mayonnaise

¼ cup Italian bread crumbs

1 cup cottage cheese

1 egg, slightly beaten

¼ tsp garlic salt

1 (8 oz) can tomato sauce

2 Tbsp Parmesan

1 cup grated mozzarella

2 small zucchini, sliced

Put peeled eggplant slices on cookie sheet. Spread with mayonnaise and crumbs. Bake at 475 degrees until brown for about 10 minutes. Remove and turn oven to 350 degrees. Mix cottage cheese, egg, and garlic salt. Layer in greased casserole all of eggplant, half of cottage cheese, half of tomato sauce, and half of parmesan and mozzarella cheese. Top with zucchini and then layer the last half of the remaining ingredients. Bake uncovered at 375 degrees for 30 minutes. Let stand for 5 minutes before cutting. Yield: 6-8 servings.

FRIED GREEN BEANS

½ cup Dijon mustard

¼ cup honey

2 tsp hot sauce

1 ½ tsp light soy sauce

Pinch of dry mustard

4 cups canola oil for frying

2 large egg whites

1 ½ cups all-purpose flour

1 ¼ cups club soda

1 lb green beans, ends trimmed

Salt to taste

In saucepan over low heat, whisk first 5 ingredients until warmed. Transfer dipping sauce to small bowl and cool. In a deep fryer or Dutch oven, heat oil. In a bowl, whisk egg whites to soft peaks. Whisk in flour and club soda. Working in batches, dip beans in batter, then lower into oil. Fry until golden brown, (about 3 minutes). Drain on paper towels; sprinkle with salt. Serve with dipping sauce.

BEEHIVES

1 box of Pillsbury Pie Refrigerator Crust (2 pie crusts)

8 large peaches

Hard sauce (recipe below)

Roll pie crusts out and cut strips 1 inch wide. Wash and dry peaches. Wrap the strips of pie crust around starting from the bottom until the peach is entirely covered. Pat and patch the crust as you go along so there are no holes. Seal the edges. Place the "beehives" on a cookie sheet and bake for 40 minutes at 400 degrees. Serve hot with hard sauce. To eat, break the "beehive" by inserting a knife and removing the stone. Spoon a heaping Tbsp of hard sauce into the cavity.

Hard Sauce:
½ stick butter

1 egg

2 cups powdered sugar

1 tsp vanilla

1 Tbsp brandy (opt)

Nutmeg

Cream butter. Add egg and mix well. Gradually work in cups of powdered sugar. Mix in vanilla. Flavor with brandy, if you like. Pile sauce into peach cavity and sprinkle with nutmeg.

*The consumption of raw or undercooked eggs may increase your risk of food-borne illness, especially to children and the elderly.

Facing page: *Mangiamo! (Let's Eat!)*
Facing page far left: *Southern Sweet Tea welcomes anyone home (Dolce!)*
Left: *Digging in to these beehives completes a perfect al fresco experience*
Below: *Our favorite Al Fresco spot on Lake Como, Italy*

MENU

Vichyssoise

Fried Green Tomato B.L.T.

Veggie Chips

Smoky Sweet Potato Salad

Fruit from the land

Luscious Lemon Squares

Blackberry Cream Tea
(the Signature Tea for Simply TeaVine)

Picnic by the Pond

A Picnic with Your Special One

Decorations: Use a bedspread or blanket, picnic basket with air-tight containers, wildflowers and fruit picked from the land, pottery mugs, and colorful napkins.

I owe a lot to my Dad. In the field beyond our backyard, he dug a hole—a deep hole. He filled it with water, stocked it with fish, and created for our family a picturesque scene of serenity and beauty. It is a picture of life and a safe haven for many of God's creatures. On any given day, one can see a beaver, turtle, snake, bird, and yes, even an alligator, enjoying the pond on the hill. The sun's reflection in the water of our pond always seems to glisten like diamonds in a treasure chest, and for a person young of heart, the shadows and sounds of the water offer an invitation to explore.

Creating a path through the open field where the family once plowed and planted, we step through the meadow filled with wildflowers, maneuvering past the blackberry's thorns, and find our way down to where the cows wade in for an afternoon dip and a cool drink. We see turtles lazily sunbathing on the logs. It is beside the pond's banks where we discover prehistoric bones of a "dinosaur" and surprise passing deer and turkey. It is at the pond, we are taught the lessons of life, overcoming our fears of squiggling worms and rusted hooks, and learning how to wait for the prize. After a day of sailing around the world, we climb the path back home with bug-bitten legs and heavy dread, yet eager to share our larger-than-life fish tales.

As teenage girls, the pond becomes our refuge—our escape spot. We luxuriate on the pond's banks, flip-flopping between suntan lotion and bug spray. The whole day stretches before us as we soak up the sun and talk about our old and new boyfriends, advising each other on how to bait the hook, lure, and catch the particular prize fish we wanted. At night, we pitch our tent by the pond and build a campfire, roasting marshmallows and sharing yet more advice on the paths we should take in life. The stars above us remind us of a world bigger than ourselves yet opens a window to dream impossible dreams.

Today we come to the pond, stake out our place on the soft grass with a bedspread, and open our basket with eager anticipation of rediscovering the simple joys and truths of life. As we sit here by the pond, we are reminded of the days of our youth. With sun in our hair, we smell the saplings and shade fragrance of the pine. We step up to the pond and look down into it, seeing our reflection of who we have become. Suddenly, we hear the plopping sound of cork in the water and see dragonflies skating across the surface. All we need are our bathing suits again and time to stand still. And it does—here by the pond.

FRIED GREEN TOMATO B.L.T.

2 firm green tomatoes, sliced into ¼ inch pieces

1 large egg, lightly beaten

½ cup buttermilk

1 Tbsp hot sauce

½ cup self-rising cornmeal mix

½ tsp salt

½ tsp pepper

½ cup all-purpose flour

Peanut or vegetable oil

6 strips bacon

Butter, softened

Kaiser rolls or sourdough bread

Remoulade sauce

Lettuce leaves

You need 2 shallow pans, one for liquid and one for dry mixture. Put sliced tomatoes into liquid mixture of egg, buttermilk, and hot sauce. Dredge in dry mixture of cornmeal, salt, pepper, and flour. Dredge again in liquid mixture and then in dry mixture. Fry tomatoes in hot oil in an iron skillet and keep warm.
Fry bacon. Drain. Butter bread and broil each side until brown in oven. Spread with remoulade sauce. Layer 3 slices fried tomatoes, 3 pieces of bacon, and lettuce on bread and add more remoulade sauce. Top with remaining bread and cut in half to serve.

Remoulade Sauce:

1 cup mayonnaise

¼ cup green onions, sliced

2 Tbsp Creole mustard

1 Tbsp parsley, chopped

1 Tbsp minced garlic

1 tsp horseradish

Stir together all ingredients. Cover and chill.

VEGGIE CHIPS

6 or more vegetables of your choice (squash, carrots, beans, beets, okra, sweet potatoes, other)

Salt

Vegetable oil

Peel vegetables. Slice as thin as you can. Place vegetables on paper towel and sprinkle lightly with salt on all sides to extract liquid from them. Let vegetables rest for 20 minutes. Then, rinse them in cold water and dry well. Heat oven to 275 degrees. Lay vegetables on a baking sheet rubbed with oil. Drizzle vegetable slices with oil. Bake 40 to 50 minutes, flipping if needed. Place cooked chips on paper towels to cool and season lightly with salt. Store in air-tight container.

LUSCIOUS LEMON SQUARES

Crust:
1 cup all-purpose flour

⅛ tsp salt

½ cup powdered sugar

1 stick butter, melted

Filling:
2 large eggs

¾ cup sugar

1 ½ Tbsp all-purpose flour

6 Tbsp lemon juice

Heat oven to 325 degrees. Spray an 8 x 8 inch baking pan with vegetable cooking spray. Put aluminum foil across pan bottom and up the sides of pan to pull bars from the pan. Spray foil. Mix dry ingredients and butter together to form dough. Press dough into pan bottom. Bake for about 20 minutes. While pastry bakes, make filling by whisking all ingredients together. Remove pan from oven and add lemon mixture. Bake for about 20 minutes until set. Let cool and then using foil handles, pull bars from pan, and set on a rack to cool. Cut into squares and serve.

SMOKY SWEET POTATO SALAD

Salad Ingredients:
3 medium sweet potatoes, smoked

½ cup dried cranberries

½ cup walnuts

½ cup chopped fresh parsley

½ cup pineapple

¼ cup celery

¼ cup red bell pepper

Dressing:
¼ cup extra-virgin olive oil

2 Tbsp pure maple syrup

2 Tbsp orange juice

2 Tbsp sherry wine vinegar or balsamic vinegar

1 Tbsp fresh lemon juice

2 tsp minced, peeled, fresh ginger

½ tsp ground cinnamon

¼ tsp ground nutmeg

1 small shallot, minced (opt)

½ tsp Dijon mustard

Romaine lettuce

Mayonnaise (opt)

Peel and cut the potatoes into quartered wedges. Smoke until tender and to desired smokiness. I use hickory chips for about 1 hour. Cool and cut into 1-inch pieces. Place in a bowl. Add salad ingredients. Mix all dressing ingredients well and add to salad mixture. Toss well. You can also add some mayonnaise for a creamy texture. Serve in a chilled bowl lined with romaine leaves. This salad can remain at room temperature up to two hours before serving. Yield: 12 servings.

Previous page: *Picnic by the Pond, "Wally" (King of our fishing hole), Wildflower Field, Turtles Sunbathing*
Left: *A gourmet Picnic*
Below: *A friendly deer on a morning outing*

Top: Spotting the rare Anhinga - a perfect picnic?
Middle: Maybe not this time.
Bottom: See you later, alligator!

Facing page:
Top: View through the cattails,
Middle: Perfect Picnic for God's creatures
  Lace cap hydrangea & Cone flowers
Bottom: Sunset over pond

VICHYSSOISE

1 can chicken broth

1 can cream of potato soup

1 cup sour cream

2 tsp minced onion

Chives, chopped

Blend broth, soup, sour cream, and onion. Chill for at least 2 hours. Garnish with chopped chives. Serves 4 to 6

MENU
Pecan Pie Muffins

Crab Crepes with Shrimp Sauce

Spinach and Strawberry Daiquiri Salad

Skillet Asparagus with Tomato Slice

Fresh Pineapple and Blackberries

Blueberry Cheesecake

A Millinery Luncheon
A Garden Luncheon with all the Accessories

Decorations: Cut the top out of a straw hat and place a hydrangea flower arrangement inside it for the centerpiece. Use handkerchiefs as napkins. Decorate the table with gloves, jewelry, and handbags to give the feel of a women's millinery store.

There's nothing more fun and powerful than for a little girl to play dress up. I remember the fond times I had as a child and relive them now in my granddaughter, who loves to put on her mother's shoes, jewelry, and makeup. What tops the occasion off, literally, is when she finds the big hat in Momma Dean's attic and puts it on. Complimented with gloves and a handbag, she becomes a model prancing down the runway. Full of self-esteem, she is bedecked and bedazzled and ready to go!

My eyes turn to a picture of my step-great-grandmother, Ms. Lena, and her sister, Ms. Lizzie, sitting in a wagon pulled by an ox. The sign on the cart reads, "Slow Train Thru Arkansaw. Don't know Ware Were Going. But On the Way." Just like my granddaughter, they are decked out with hats and handbags and much assurance that they are going places—and important places at that.

Throughout the ages, headwear for women has been an essential item to complete a wardrobe. It might be as simple as a ribbon or a fancy clasp, but it has always served as a necessary tool to keep the hair in place and promote the fashion of the time. In the early 1900s, very few women worked outside the home. Ms. Lena, however, was an exception. To help with the family's livelihood, she worked in a millinery shop in downtown Hattiesburg. The shop not only provided fashionable hats for women, but also important accessories to complete an outfit such as hatpins, gloves, and handbags. I can just see my great-grandmother coming home to the cabin from a day's work at the hat shop and telling the family what the women of Hattiesburg were wearing to keep up with the times.

Throughout the ages, hats have changed in style but have always been the most noticeable accessory fashion item anyone can wear. The old saying goes, "If you want to get ahead and get noticed, then get a hat." Indeed the word "ahead" means just that—one head further forward. The shop where my great-grandmother worked would have offered enormous, elaborate hats with feathers, flowers, ribbons, and tulle for those special outings. Yet, at the cabin home, simple cotton bonnets were put on to keep the hot sun off the woman's face for daily chores of farm life. In the 1920s, my grandmother wore the cloche, which hugged the head to show off the shorter hair of the time, or for parties, the "flapper girl" band around the head with a single feather. In the 1950s, my mom wore hats only for special occasions, such as going to church, weddings, or teas. As children, my sister and I were always proud to parade our new Easter dresses and hats, complimented with gloves and black patent leather shoes. Even today, putting on a sun hat for the beach makes a woman feel "special."

Little girls have not changed too much throughout the years, and neither have big girls. We still love to play dress up, and a garden luncheon tea is the perfect place to go bold and beautiful. Our menu is light and perfect for the season, and ladies will love indulging in these scrumptious dishes. The spinach and Strawberry Daiquiri Salad gives a festive feel to start off the party. Crepes in any form fancy up a meal, and our delicious Crab Crepes with Shrimp Sauce bring the summer season to the table. To dress up the plate, we accessorize by adding the color of pineapple and fresh tomatoes, asparagus, and berries from the garden. We complete the meal with a Blueberry Cheesecake that is rich and creamy, yet contains only a fraction of the fat of a regular cheesecake. The ladies of this luncheon tea will be giving a hats off to the hostess for bringing out the little girl in all of us!

PECAN PIE MUFFINS

2 eggs

⅔ cup butter, softened

1 cup brown sugar

½ cup flour

1 cup of finely chopped pecans

Cream eggs and softened butter. Add dry ingredients. Mix and fill small greased muffin tins about ¾ full. Bake at 325 degrees for 15 to 18 minutes.

Previous page: *Salad and accessories, Women with their hats*
Clockwise from above: *Brass Mesh Handbag (c. 1930), Hats from O'Ferrill's millinery shop in Hattiesburg, MS (c. 1900), Sisters going places, Dressing up the table, Delicious Savory Crepes, A toast to hats!*

CRAB CREPES WITH SHRIMP SAUCE

Basic Crepes:

1 cup plus 2 Tbsp all-purpose flour

1 ½ cups milk

3 eggs

1 Tbsp butter, melted

⅛ tsp salt

Vegetable oil

Combine all ingredients except vegetable oil in electric blender until smooth. Refrigerate batter for 1 to 2 hours. Brush the bottom of a 6- inch crepe pan or heavy skillet with vegetable oil; place pan over medium heat until oil is just hot, not smoking. Pour 3 Tbsp batter into pan; quickly tilt pan in all directions so that batter covers the pan in a thin film. Cook about 1 minute. Lift edge of crepe to test for doneness. Crepe is ready for flipping when it can be shaken loose from the pan. Flip the crepe and cook about 30 seconds on the other side. This side is where the filling is placed. Place on a towel to cool. Stack between layers of waxed paper to prevent sticking. Repeat until all batter is used. Yield: 10 crepes

Crab Filling:

1 pound lump crabmeat, drained

1 cup finely chopped celery

½ cup mayonnaise

¼ cup chopped green onions with tops

2 tsp lemon juice

1 (2 oz) jar diced pimento, drained

½ tsp curry powder

Combine all ingredients in a bowl. Spread 2 Tbsp of crab mixture evenly over each crepe; roll up, and place seam side down in a lightly greased 9 x 13 inch baking dish. Bake, covered, at 350 degrees for 25 minutes or until thoroughly heated. Place crepes on serving dishes and spoon shrimp sauce over crepes. Yield: 2 crepes each for 5 people.

Shrimp Sauce:

¼ cup butter

¼ cup all-purpose flour

2 cups milk

1 cup chopped, shrimp, peeled and cooked

2 tsp lemon juice

1 ½ tsp tomato paste

½ tsp salt

⅛ tsp red pepper

Melt butter in a heavy saucepan over low heat; add flour, stirring until smooth. Cook 1 minute, stirring constantly. Gradually add milk; cook over medium heat, stirring constantly, until thickened and bubbly. Add remaining ingredients; mix well. Continue to cook over medium heat until thoroughly heated. Serve immediately. Yield: about 2 cups.

SPINACH AND STRAWBERRY DAIQUIRI SALAD

¼ cup lime juice

¼ cup honey

¼ tsp poppy seeds

¼ tsp Dijon mustard

¼ cup vegetable oil

1 cup sliced almonds

¼ tsp salt

¼ cup white sugar

1 (10 oz) bag baby spinach

2 pints sliced fresh strawberries

1 cup toasted flaked coconut

½ red onion, sliced

Combine the lime juice, honey, poppy seeds, and mustard in a small bowl; slowly whisk in the oil. Combine the almonds, salt, and sugar in a large skillet. Stir constantly over low heat until almonds are light golden brown (about 5 minutes). Remove nuts from the skillet to cool. Toss the spinach, strawberries, coconut, onions, and cooled almonds in a large bowl. Top with prepared dressing, and toss.

SKILLET ASPARAGUS WITH TOMATO SLICE

2 pounds fresh asparagus, trimmed

2 tbsp unsalted butter

Salt

Tomato slices

Garnish:
Lemon wedges

Slice of hard-boiled egg (opt)

Wash asparagus. Melt butter in skillet and place asparagus with a little water. Cover and cook over medium heat for 5 minutes. Time will vary according to how thick asparagus is. Season to taste. Place tomato slice on plate and top with asparagus. Garnish with lemon wedge or slice of boiled egg (opt).

FRESH PINEAPPLE AND BLACKBERRIES

Fresh pineapple

Blackberries

Mint

Cut green top off pineapple and slit vertically in half. Cut each half lengthwise into two pieces. Cut pineapple into pieces and place in bowl. Top with fresh blackberries and mint.

BLUEBERRY CHEESECAKE

1 cup graham cracker crumbs

3 tbsp butter, melted

1 tbsp sugar

2 (8 oz) packages ½ less fat cream cheese

1 (8 oz) package fat free cream cheese

1 cup sugar

3 tbsp all-purpose flour

½ tsp salt

2 large eggs

2 egg whites

1 (8 oz) container light sour cream

1 tsp vanilla extract

1 ½ cups fresh or frozen blueberries

1 cup fat-free frozen whipped topping

¼ cup sour cream

Clockwise from below: *Let the fashion show begin, Family Vintage Jewelry (c. 1900), Swan "Ms Sippy" (showing off her hat), A Milliner's Delight, Fruit - A cool compliment to any meal!*

Combine graham cracker crumbs, butter, and sugar in a small bowl. Press mixture on bottom and sides of a 9-inch spring-form pan coated with cooking spray. Bake at 350 degrees for 5 minutes. Remove from oven and set aside. Beat cream cheeses at medium speed with an electric mixer until smooth. Combine sugar, flour, and salt. Add to cream cheese, beating until blended. Add eggs, 1 at a time, beating well after each addition. Add egg whites, beating until blended. Add container of sour cream and vanilla, beating just until blended. Gently stir in blueberries. Pour mixture into prepared pan. Bake at 300 degrees for 1 hour and 10 minutes or until center of cheesecake is firm. Turn off oven, and let cheesecake stand in oven, with oven door partially open for 30 minutes. Remove cheesecake from oven and cool in pan on a wire rack for 30 minutes. Cover cheesecake and chill 8 hours. Release sides of pan. Stir together whipped topping and sour cream. Spread over cheesecake.

Fall

Game Day Spread
A TAILGATE PARTY TO KICK OFF THE SEASON

Ladies Luncheon on the Lawn
A SOUTHERN FOOD LUNCHEON TEA

Dinner on the Boards
"OLD SOUTH STYLE"

A Festival of Food
A MENU HONORING FAMOUS MISSISSIPPIANS

A Thiskamas Affair
A HOLIDAY HARVEST WITH NEW TRADITIONS

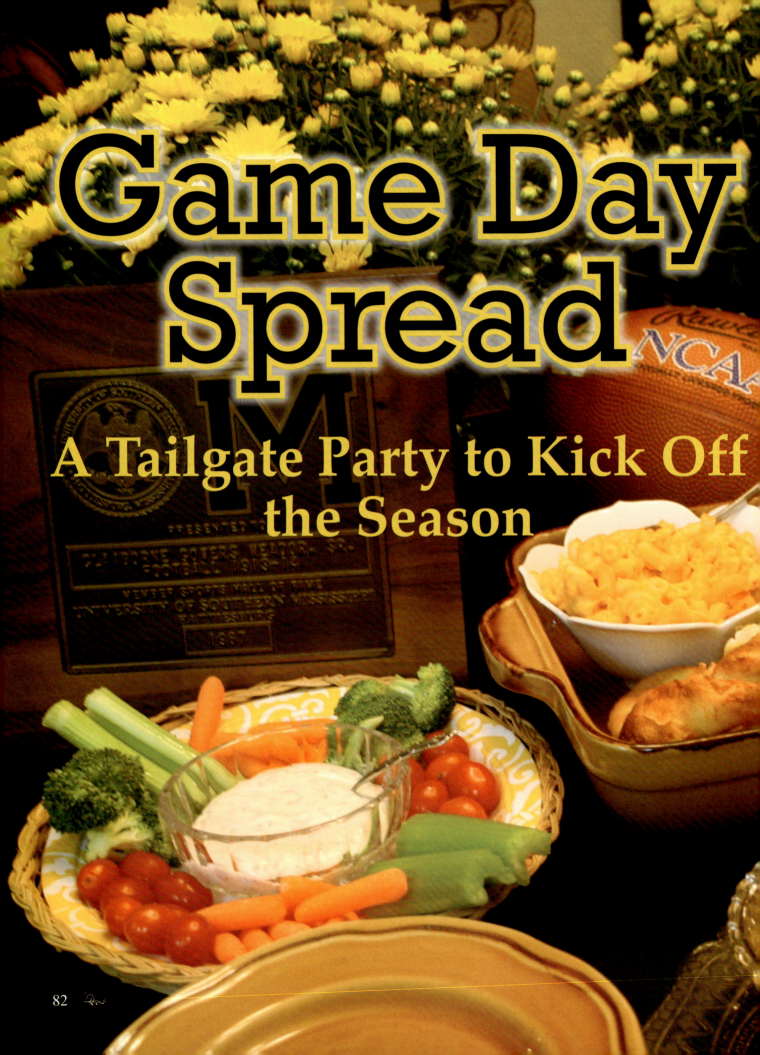

Menu

Cynthia's Family Reunion Dip

Vegetables and Curry Vegetable Dip

Dad's Pimento and Cheese

Nancy's Fruit and Fruit Dip

Chess Pie with Blackberries

Southern Fried Chicken

Erin's Stuffed Eggs

Chocolate Fudge Cupcakes

Black-eyed Susan Tea

Decorations: Adorn the table with linen and dinnerware, mascot logo items, and flowers of the school colors. If available, use pictures of family and friends from their time at the school. The story of USM's school colors goes all the way back to the school's beginning. A committee was chosen in 1912 to decide the colors. On the way to the meeting, one of the members saw a wide field of black-eyed susans and was so impressed that she convinced the group to adopt the colors of these flowers. After a student body election, black and gold were designated the official school colors and have been so ever since.

The squad had only 15 members, and organizers had to work hard to get even that many since few potential players understood the game. Claiborne Gowers Meador, my grandfather, was one of them. After graduating from Hattiesburg High School in 1912, and eager to begin a new chapter of life, he literally jumped right into the football team at the new school up the road-Mississippi Normal College. The team had lots of spirit, he told me, even though they were not very good. They played boy scout teams, high schools, and military academies, and only won one game, but the bond and the memories they created with each other lasted throughout all their lives. The Normalites played at Kamper Park, the city park the Meador family had helped clear, and right beside my family's old home on Hardy Street before they moved to the cabin. Students would walk the mile or so from the school, and later, ride the trolley down what was then the longest street in the United States to the games. My grandfather told me the best player on the team only had one arm. When he would catch the ball, he would mockingly wave his stump in opponents' faces. And they all had nicknames for how they played the game. I remember Pa talking about "Shorty," "Blink," and "Strut." My grandfather's nickname was "Spider" because he looked like a spider monkey when he played. He was very thin and gangly, but fast. I asked him how he could play on a football team being so thin, and he replied, "They just used me as their punching bag." His nickname stuck with him all his life.

Interstate rivalry was born between Ole Miss and Normal, now the University of Southern Mississippi. A large crowd gathered to witness the Rebels, the team from Mississippi's oldest state-supported institution, defeat the squad from the youngest state-supported institution by a score of 13-7. Normal finished the year at 1-5-1, and my grandfather was inducted into the university's Sports Hall of Fame in 1967. As you can see, the game is entrenched in our hearts, so much that other Meador family members have cheered and played on the team at Southern Miss.

How fun it is to bundle yourself up in a blanket when the first cold snap comes in the fall. You can drink hot chocolate, tea, or a hot toddy, and yell your team on to victory. And there's nothing better than to kick off the season with a tailgate party. I have included a fantabulous Fruit dip from my sister who wore the black and gold as a cheerleader, stuffed Eggs from my daughter, the homecoming queen, and my dad's favorite Pimento and cheese sandwich. Although he never attended USM, he was an avid fan and supporter for the team, serving as the first president for The Century Club at the university. The food on our menu is food that can be prepared ahead of time, so everyone can just sit back and enjoy the game!

CYNTHIA'S FAMILY REUNION DIP

1 cup grated Cracker Barrel extra sharp cheddar cheese

1 cup Kraft pre-shredded cheddar cheese

5 green onions, chopped

¼ cup jalapenos, sliced and chopped (discard seeds)

2 cans of Mexicorn (drain)

1 cup sour cream

1 cup mayonnaise

Garlic salt

Cayenne pepper (opt)

Frito Lay scoops

Grate cheese. (Cynthia grated Cracker Barrel extra sharp cheese and added a bag of already-grated Kraft cheddar cheese.) Chop green onions and remove seeds from jalapenos. Mix all, except cayenne pepper, together. Sprinkle cayenne pepper on top for color (optional). Serve with Frito scoops.

Previous page: A Gameday Spread
Top: USM Meador Alumni
Bottom: Sports Hall of Fame gives thumbs up to C.G. Meador, member of 1st football team in 1912

DAD'S PIMENTO AND CHEESE

1 lb sharp cheddar cheese, finely grated

¾ cup mayonnaise

1 jar pimentos, drained

1 tsp grated onions (opt)

Garlic salt

Pepper

Wheat bread

Grate cheese finely. Add mayonnaise to desired consistency. Fold in pimentos, onions, and add spices. Spread on bread.

VEGETABLES AND CURRY VEGETABLE DIP

Assorted raw vegetables such as cauliflower florets, carrot sticks, sliced squash and zucchini, celery sticks, and cherry tomatoes

Dip:

1 pint mayonnaise

1 Tbsp celery seed

2 small cloves garlic, minced

1 Tbsp prepared horseradish

3-4 tsp Lea & Perrins

2 tsp curry powder

2 tsp mustard

2 Tbsp fresh lemon juice

Mix ingredients and chill at least 12 hours. This dip is delicious with raw vegetables.

Top & Middle: *Dips are a must on Gameday*

NANCY'S FRUIT AND FRUIT DIP

Fresh pineapple and fruit of the season, cut up, and Toothpicks

Dip:

1 (7 oz) Kraft marshmallow crème

1 (8 oz) pkg cream cheese

3 Tbsp pineapple juice

Cut fruit and arrange on platter. Mix marshmallow crème, cream cheese, and juice for dip. Place in pineapple shell or bowl to serve. Decorate with pineapple top. Serve with toothpicks.

SOUTHERN FRIED CHICKEN

1-2 ½ lb chicken, cut up

Lawry's seasoned salt

3 eggs

⅓ cup water

2 cups self-rising flour

1 tsp pepper

Crisco Shortening for frying

After chicken is cut up, season with seasoned salt. Let chicken sit in fridge for 2 to 3 hours. Beat eggs with water. In a separate bowl, mix self-rising flour and pepper. Dip seasoned chicken in egg; coat well in flour mixture. Fry in a Dutch oven in moderately hot shortening (about 350 degrees) until brown and crisp. Dark meat should be cooked for 13-14 minutes. White meat should be cooked for 8-10 minutes.

Top: The ultimate "Southern" comfort food - fried chicken!
Bottom: Black-Eyed Susans and chess pie (Black and Gold Forever!)

CHESS PIE WITH BLACKBERRIES

1 9-inch pie crust

½ stick unsalted butter

½ cup sugar

5 egg yolks

1 Tbsp flour

2 cups milk

Sauce:

2 cups (10 oz) fresh or frozen blackberries

¼ cup sugar

2 Tbsp lemon juice

1 Tbsp dark rum

Make dough or use a 9-inch pie crust. Set aside. Cream the butter and sugar together until light. Beat in yolks all at once. Mix in flour well. Stir in milk and mix well. Pour into crust and bake at 350 degrees for about 1 hour, or until set and lightly browned. For sauce, combine berries, sugar, and lemon juice in a small saucepan. Simmer over low heat for about 15 minutes. Stir in rum. You can freeze this sauce and thaw before serving. Serve pie either hot or cold.
Note: May substitute blueberries or raspberries for school colors.

ERIN'S STUFFED EGGS

1 dozen eggs

4 Tbsp mayonnaise

2 ½ Tbsp dill relish

2 Tbsp yellow mustard

⅛ tsp cayenne

¼ tsp horseradish

Salt and pepper to taste

Paprika

Put eggs in water and bring to a boil. Turn heat off and leave eggs in water for 10 minutes. Take eggs out of water, cool, and peel. Cut egg in ½ and put yolk in a separate bowl. Mix egg yolk with mayo, dill relish, mustard, cayenne, horseradish, salt, and pepper. Spoon yolk mixture into hard egg whites. Sprinkle paprika for garnish.

CHOCOLATE FUDGE CUPCAKES

1 ¾ cup sugar

1 cup flour

4 eggs

4 squares unsweetened chocolate

2 sticks margarine

2 cups chopped pecans (opt)

2 tsp vanilla

Basic Decorator Icing

Combine sugar and flour. Add eggs and blend. Don't beat. In a double boiler, melt chocolate and margarine. Add nuts and stir. Combine chocolate mixture, vanilla, and flour mixture. Do not beat. Put in muffins tins. Bake at 325 degrees for about 25 minutes.

Decorate with Basic Decorator Icing (page 54) and food coloring for school colors. Yield: 24 cupcakes.

BLACK-EYED SUSAN TEA
from
SIMPLY TEAVINE TEA ROOM
(SIGNATURE TEA FOR USM)

Top: Here's our girl again at homecoming!
Middle: Erin's awesome eggs
Bottom: Go USM!
Bottom right: B&B guests always enjoy a chocolate treat

Facing page: Clockwise from Upper-left: Mother & daughters share the same school spirit, Nancy Meador (Miss USM, Homecoming court), Cousin John carries on the family football tradition, Cheering on my daughter, the Queen!, Nancy keeping "Southern" spirits high!

Clockwise from above: C.G. Meador HOF induction ('67), Homecoming parade (a perfect place to people watch), A Young C.G. Meador (1912), Golden Eagle (mascot of USM), Early football attire. A collage of the Meador family members at USM…from football players to beauties & queens to lifelong fans

Ladies Luncheon On The Lawn
A Southern Food Luncheon Tea

MENU

Black-eyed Pea Dip

Ginger and Honey Sweet Tea

Paradise Chicken Salad on Croissant

Cheese Delights

Fresh Fruit with Dressing

Almond and Orange Green Salad

Turbinado Strawberry Shortcakes with Cream

Decorations: Use vintage teacups with flowers as table favors and for decorations. A collection of mismatched china patterns will create a whimsical effect for a ladies' gathering.

Today the Meador Homestead cabin sits quietly, oblivious to its new South surroundings of fast food restaurants, factories, and major highways. The cabin has gotten lost in time, thank goodness, and knows nothing about televisions, telephones, or social media. It relies on an era when people really knew their neighbors and depended on them. But even an unfamiliar face is welcome. The people who show up on the doorsteps can be family, friends, or strangers. In fact, the stranger within our door is one of our greatest joys. All are welcome to come in, sit a spell, and even have a good old Southern meal on the hand hewn board table. The meal doesn't have to be elaborate to warrant the occasion to just get together for some good conversation and a cup of tea.

Ladies have gathered at the cabin to enjoy Southern hospitality after a club meeting or Bible study, before a day of playing bridge in the parlor, or after weekend chores are done. There have been large groups enjoying a bridal tea, anniversary party, or garden club. There have been ladies alone, getting away from the busy world to de-stress with a cup of the hot, black brew. Writers find that the writer's block they have had has gone away just within a few minutes of rocking on the porch or sitting in front of the old cabin fireplace. There have been appreciation lunches for employees, spiritual retreats, family gatherings, and birthday celebrations.

The Meador Homestead cabin is as it has always been---open for anyone to come in, find a little peace, and share in the leisurely pace of an era that is quickly passing us by. Ladies can experience the old and new way of sharing Southern hospitality and its food around a common table that will only bring the strong bonds of camaraderie.

Nothing is more traditional in the South than chicken salad, black-eyed peas, cheese straws, and iced tea. We have a fresh way to serve our peas with our Black-eyed Pea dip. The Chicken salad is Simply TeaVine's tearoom signature dish and brainchild. Focus on this single dish and success is assured for any luncheon. Because the fragrance of a hot croissant can be the best lunchtime greeting, we serve the salad tucked inside the warm bread.

Fresh fruit becomes fancy with a sauce to adorn it, and the green salad with oranges brings a tanginess and spirit to the party. The Cheese Delight recipe has been passed down for many generations in my family and a staple for a true Southern lady "get-together." We finish our meal with strawberry shortcake sprinkled with turbinado sugar for the perfect dessert to serve to friends in the cool shade on the lawn.

All you need now is to add long-time friends and conversation and you have a typical Southern Belle ladies luncheon. With this menu, you have mastered the art of the "get together" and true Southern hospitality! Congratulations!

BLACK-EYED PEA DIP

4 (15 oz) cans black-eyed peas, rinsed and drained

1 cup chopped green bell pepper

1 cup chopped yellow bell pepper

1 cup chopped red bell pepper

1 cup chopped red onion

1 ½ cups cherry tomatoes, halved

1 cup finely chopped fresh parsley

Chips, crackers, or Frito scoops

Place peas in a large bowl. Add all bell peppers, onions, tomatoes, and parsley. Pour dressing over top and toss well. Cover and refrigerate for at least 2 hours before serving. For appetizer, we place two Frito scoops on a plate and fill with dip.

Dressing:

¾ cup balsamic vinegar

½ cup extra virgin olive oil

2 tsp salt

1 tsp black pepper

¼ cup sugar

Whisk ingredients together.

GINGER AND HONEY SWEET TEA

3 cups water

2 family-size tea bags

½ cup honey

1 Tbsp grated fresh ginger

7 cups cold water

Bring 3 cups water to a boil and add tea bags. Boil 1 minute and remove from heat. Cover and steep for 10 minutes. Discard tea bags. Add honey, stirring until dissolved. Pour into a 1 gallon container and add ginger and 7 cups cold water. Serve over ice. Garnish with lemon slices, if desired.

Previous page: *Southern hospitality at its best*
Clockwise from above: *A perfect lunch on the lawn, Lunch with friends, Wax Begonias, Fresh fruit dressing*

PARADISE CHICKEN SALAD ON CROISSANT

6 chicken breasts (8 cups) chicken, cooked and diced

Reserve chicken stock to cook rice

6 green onions

4 celery stalks

2 Granny Smith apples

2 cups red grapes (cut in quarters)

⅓ cup chopped pecans or walnuts (opt)

1 cup Uncle Ben's long grain and wild rice

Croissants for sandwiches

Chop chicken, onions, celery, apples, grapes, and pecans in a food processor and then combine. Cook rice in broth and add to chicken mixture. Yield: 12 servings

Sauce for Salad:

6 heaping Tbsp chutney

6 heaping Tbsp mayonnaise

2 heaping Tbsp sour cream

6 Tbsp chicken broth from cooked chicken

4 tsp honey

2 Tbsp lemon juice

1 tsp salt

1 tsp pepper

1 tsp nutmeg

Mix sauce ingredients for salad and stir dressing in with chicken mixture. Spoon chicken salad onto a croissant and enjoy paradise!

CHEESE DELIGHTS

2 lbs cheese, grated (1 lb sharp, 1 lb medium)

1 tsp salt

½ lb butter, melted

1 tsp cayenne pepper

4 cups sifted flour

Mix ingredients and work until it is like putty. Put through cookie press in your favorite shape or shape in logs and slice. Bake at 350 degrees for about 20 minutes or until light brown. Yield: 50 to 75 cheese delights.

FRESH FRUIT WITH DRESSING

1 watermelon, cut up

2 cantaloupes, cut up

1 honeydew, cut up

3 (16 oz) cans pineapple chunks, drained

4 pts strawberries

6 sliced bananas, covered with pineapple juice

⅓ lb red seedless grapes

⅓ lb green seedless grapes

Fruit salad dressing (opt)

Cut melons into pieces. Remove all seeds. Drain all pineapple chunks and reserve juice. Remove greens from strawberries. Leave small strawberries whole and cut large ones. Slice bananas and cover with pineapple juice. Pull all seedless grapes from stems. Store fruit in separate containers until ready to mix. Mix all fruit together. Serve with fruit salad dressing for those who desire it. Serves 25 people.

Fruit Salad Dressing:

⅓ cup sugar

4 tsp cornstarch

¼ tsp salt

Juice of 1 lemon

Juice of 1 orange

1 cup unsweetened pineapple juice

2 eggs

2 (3 oz) pkgs cream cheese, whipped

In a double boiler, mix sugar, cornstarch, and salt. Add lemon juice, orange juice, and pineapple juice. Cook over warm water for 20 minutes, stirring constantly. Beat eggs and temper them before adding to hot mixture in order to prevent scrambling the eggs and causing lumps. To temper, add a little cooked mixture to the eggs slowly, stirring constantly until well blended. Repeat process and blend well. Then slowly add to mixture in the double boiler, stirring constantly. Cook, stirring 5 minutes more. Strain contents to remove any lumps. Cool and blend with cream cheese. Serve over fruit.

ALMOND AND ORANGE GREEN SALAD

Romaine lettuce

Slivered almonds

¼ cup sugar

6 green onion tops, chopped (opt)

Bacon bits

1 (11 oz) can mandarin oranges

Tear and chill lettuce. Combine almonds and sugar in saucepan and stir until sugar is brown. Cool mixture on wax paper. Combine lettuce, almond mixture, green onions, bacon bits, and oranges. Toss with dressing. Yield: 6 to 8 servings.

Dressing:

1 cup vegetable oil

¼ cup vinegar

¼ cup sugar

1 tsp salt

Dash red and black pepper

1 Tbsp parsley flakes

Combine all ingredients for dressing and chill.

Clockwise from left: A perfect spot for friendly conversation, Strawberry shortcakes - How sweet it is!

TURBINADO STRAWBERRY SHORTCAKES WITH CREAM

2 cups flour

1 Tbsp sugar

3 tsp baking powder

⅓ cup unsalted butter

1 egg, beaten

⅔ cup milk or cream

Cream for brushing

Turbinado (raw sugar)

Cut strawberries, sprinkled with sugar and orange juice

Whipped cream

Preheat oven to 450 degrees. Sift together dry ingredients. Cut in butter with a pastry blender until mixture resembles coarse crumbs. Combine egg and milk; add all at once to flour mixture. Stir just to moisten. Lightly flour hands and form dough into 6-8 biscuits. Lightly brush tops with heavy cream and sprinkle with turbinado sugar. Bake on ungreased baking sheet for 10 minutes, until golden on top and firm to the touch. Let cool. (Shortcakes can be stored in an airtight container for up to 2 days.) To serve, halve shortcakes horizontally with a serrated knife. Place bottom on plate, top with berries, a dollop of whipped cream, and remaining shortcake halves. Top with another dollop of cream. You can serve also with strawberry or chocolate sauce. Serves 8.

Below: *Drinking sweet tea-the nectar of the South*
Facing page: *Red Hat Ladies enjoying their lunch on the lawn, A Southern Belle and her flowers*

Our "Old South" Menu
(Southern Cookin' at Its Best)

Iron Skillet Cornbread • Crabmeat Bisque

Champagne Punch • Honey-Baked Ham

Fricasseed Chicken over Rice • Old Southern "Cawn Puddin"

Buttered Peas • Turnip Greens

Black-eyed Peas—Plantation Style • Georgia's Pecan Pie

Old Virginia Sweet Potato Pie • Election "Rum" Cake

Fruit, Nuts, and Chocolates • Plantation Tea

Famous Mint Julep From Old Southern Tea Room • Wine

Dinner on the Boards
"Old South Style"

Decorations: Use any historical pieces from the Civil War era. We used family silverware and china that dated back to 1861. Family water goblets were from the time period. We also used tin photographs taken of the family. A pineapple and celery stalks in glass containers are staple ornaments for the sideboard or table showing hospitality and wealth.

We've all seen the Hollywood movies showing the grandeur living style of the plantations in the South. In reality, most Southerners lived quietly on small farms in wooden-framed houses or in log cabins such as our 1884 dogtrot home. They rarely owned slaves; 63% of the farmers in southeast Mississippi owned no slaves. If they did, it was a husband and wife team working alongside their owner. All levels of society, however, shared the same culinary roots and distinctive style of food. And Southerners knew how to entertain. Traveling from place to place often took days, so guests frequently stayed for several days at a time, if not weeks. Lavish dinners were served on beautiful tables brought over from Europe, designed to show off the hosts' hospitality and abundance of the plantation. The Southern family farm would do the same thing in a different way. In the dogtrot, boards would be laid atop wooden saw horses and all would gather around a plentiful feast. Travelers knew that bed and board was always waiting for them. The food was unassuming but plentiful. Where some plantation homes were known to serve at least 29 courses at the 2:00 p.m. dinnertime, the farm homes served what was available, and the rich soil of the South gave them much to choose from.

A typical pre-Civil War Southern plantation dinner would begin with the serving of the bread, and cornbread was the staple. The Indians grew corn virtually year-round, giving us grits, hominy, and corn dishes, along with sweet potatoes, beans, and squash. They introduced us to crawfish and shrimp, thus the seafood second course. Punch and wine was served every 3rd course. I have included old recipes for spiked punch and mint juleps. Because of the lack of refrigeration, the meat course was small animals such as turkey, baby pigs, chicken, quail, and squirrels. The African slave brought along with them the method of rolling food in corn meal and deep frying. Our "Fricasseed Chicken" was a typical way to serve chicken and a personal favorite recipe of Abraham Lincoln. Following the meat course would come a plethora of vegetables grown on the land. We have chosen to serve turnip greens, rice, peas, squash casserole, and corn. Desserts would be offered such as our sweet potato and pecan pies and Abraham Lincoln's Election or "Rum" Cake. After dinner, everything would be removed from the table, and fruit, nuts, and

chocolates would be served. The ladies would retire to the parlor, cigars and cordials brought out to the men, and lively discussions of the war ahead would ensue.

After that typical dinner, I'm sure none of the men thought the Confederacy would collapse because it would not be able to feed its people. Mississippi seceded in 1861, and my great-great-grandfather became a part of the war serving as a chaplain. He lost an arm at the Siege of Vicksburg and, like the South, never was the same.

What did not change, however, was the food. It is still as satisfying and warming now as it was on those long-ago days when the houses and the great trees were young. Around our boards, the "Old South" still lives! Enjoy!

Previous page: Georgias Pie, Rockin', Playin' & Eatin' - totally southern

IRON SKILLET CORNBREAD

1 cup yellow cornmeal

1 cup plain flour

½ teaspoon sugar

4 tsp. baking powder

½ tsp salt

½ cup safflower oil or bacon drippings

1 egg

1 ½ cup milk, approximately

Place a large cast-iron skillet in the oven and turn temperature to 400 degrees. While the oven and the pan are preheating, mix dry ingredients in a bowl. Mix oil, egg, and milk, and then stir into dry ingredients. Add a bit more milk if batter is stiff. Remove skillet from the oven. Grease quickly with vegetable oil or bacon fat and pour the batter in, smoothing with a spatula if necessary. Bake about 20 minutes at 350 degrees, until golden brown. Serve hot from the skillet.
Serves 6 to 8 people.

TURNIP GREENS

6 bunches turnip greens

4 slices bacon

2 tbsp sugar

½ tsp salt

½ tsp pepper

½ cup water

Strip the leaves from the stems. Immerse leaves in water. In an iron skillet, fry bacon over low heat for about 7 minutes. Carefully lift greens from the water and add to the skillet. Turn several times. Add sugar, seasonings, and water. Simmer over very low heat for 3 hours. Remove from liquid and serve hot. Serves 6.

CRABMEAT BISQUE

½ lb. fresh mushrooms, sliced

3 Tbsp minced green onion

6 Tbsp butter

¼ cup flour

3 ½ cups milk

1 cup chicken broth

1 lb. lump crabmeat, drained

1 Tbsp seasoned salt

¾ tsp ground mace

⅛ tsp cayenne pepper

½ tsp hot sauce

¼ cup sherry

Saute mushrooms and onion in butter. Stir in flour. Gradually add milk and broth, stirring constantly, until slightly thickened. Add crabmeat and seasonings. Serve immediately. Yields 8 servings.

BUTTERED PEAS

2 lbs large green peas (3 cups)

7 to 8 qts. water

1 ½ tsp salt

1 to 2 Tbsp sugar

¼ tsp salt

6 Tbsp butter

Drop peas in boiling salted water. Boil uncovered for 5 to 10 minutes. Drain. Add sugar, salt, and butter to peas. Turn into a hot vegetable dish and serve as soon as possible.

HONEY BAKED HAM

Traditional bone-in butt half ham

6 oz ginger ale

1 can pineapples in heavy syrup

Toothpicks

Dark brown sugar (to taste)

Nutmeg

Cinnamon

Parsley and apples for garnish

Rinse ham and place in baking pan. Pour ginger ale over ham. Pin pineapples to ham with toothpicks. Mix brown sugar with heavy syrup from can of pineapples and pour over the ham. Sprinkle ham with nutmeg and cinnamon (about a Tbsp. of each). Use a spoon to evenly mix the mixture in the bottom of the pan. Cover with foil and bake. Normally bake 25 min. for each pound at 325 degrees. Garnish with parsley and apples.

GEORGIA'S PECAN PIE

Pastry:

½ cup Crisco

1 ½ cup flour

1 tsp salt

3 or 4 Tbsp cold water

Filling:

3 eggs-beaten

1 cup sugar

1 cup light Karo

1 stick melted butter

1 tsp vanilla

1 cup pecans (broken coarsely)

Make pastry and put in pie pan. Put in liquid mixture. Bake at 250 degrees for 1 hour or until golden brown.

Clockwise from below: Succulent ham, Champagne Punch, Food "on the board", Southern Skillet Corn Bread

OLD SOUTHERN "CAWN PUDDIN"

3 Tbsp butter

3 Tbsp flour

1 Tbsp sugar

¾ tsp salt

¾ cup milk

1 (17 oz) can cream-style corn

3 eggs

Melt butter in a saucepan. Add flour, sugar, and salt until smooth. Cook 1 minute. Gradually add milk, heat, and stir until thick. Stir in corn. In a separate bowl, beat eggs well. Add to pan stirring constantly. Pour in 1 ½ qt. baking dish. Bake at 350 degrees for 1 hour. Yields 6 servings.

BLACK-EYED PEAS— PLANTATION STYLE

Peas

Ham hock

Water

1 hot pepper

Black pepper

Dash of Lea & Perrin

Pinch of sugar

2 pods whole okra

Sprinkle parsley

Sprinkle paprika

2 white onion rings

Put peas in cold water. Let come to a boil; have the ham hock boiling in separate pot. Pour off water from peas, and put in the boiling meat-water, adding the hot pepper. Season with black pepper, a dash of Lea & Perrin, and a pinch of sugar. Boil until peas are tender. Place in serving dish and top with okra, a sprinkle of parsley and paprika, and 2 white onion rings.

Clockwise from near right: *Family china (c, 1861), Long-time Symbol of hospitaly. Tea on the boards (Simply Teavine style). Reading on the boards*

FRICASSEED CHICKEN OVER RICE

(Recipe from *The First Ladies Cookbook* and a favorite dish of Abraham Lincoln)

2 to 3 fryers, cut up

Salt and pepper

Flour for dredging

Lard or butter for frying chicken and Parsley

1/2 pint cream

1/4 tsp nutmeg

1/4 tsp mace

A little butter rolled in flour and parsley sprigs

cooked rice

Cut up chicken into pieces of desired size. Wipe dry, season with flour and pepper and dredge lightly with flour. Fry them in lard or butter until brown. Take out of pan, and keep hot in warmer. Skim the gravy in the frying pan, and pour the cream into it. Season with nutmeg, mace, butter, and parsley. Pour gravy over chicken pieces and serve over cooked rice.

OLD VIRGINIA SWEET POTATO PIE

1 large sweet potato

2 eggs

1/2 cup sugar

2 tbsp butter

2 tbsp cream

pinch of salt

1 cup milk

1/4 cup sherry wine

To the cooked potato, add eggs, sugar, butter, cream, and pinch of salt. Beat until smooth. Add the milk; stir and add the sherry. Put into 9-inch pastry pie shell and bake in 400 degree oven for 10 minutes. Decrease oven temperature to 325 degrees and bake for about 20 minutes longer, or until custard is set. Remove from oven and cool. Garnish with sweetened whipped cream, flavored with sherry.

Above: *Lincoln's favorite chicken*
Left: *Sweet Potato Pie, Oh, how sweet!*

FAMOUS MINT JULEP FROM *OLD SOUTHERN TEA ROOM*

For each serving:

2 Sprigs fresh mint

1 rounded tsp powdered sugar

Few drops of water

2 jiggers bourbon whiskey, divided

Crushed ice

Sprig of fresh mint for garnish

Powdered sugar (opt)

Put 2 sprigs of fresh mint in bottom of tall thin glass. Add 1 rounded tsp. powdered sugar and a few drops of water. Use a wooden muddler, and bruise the mint with the sugar and the water, thoroughly. Pour in jigger of bourbon whiskey. Pack the glass to brim with finely crushed ice. One more jigger of the whiskey. Let trickle to bottom of glass. Put sprig of fresh mint in top of glass and serve with two straws. (If desired, top sprig of mint can be dipped in finely powdered sugar while damp.)

CHAMPAGNE PUNCH

(Old Vicksburg Wedding Reception Recipe from *Old Southern Tea Room*)

3 quarts champagne

1 quart Carbonated Water

1 tea-cup of rum

Pour over 2 quart-blocks strong frozen unsweetened lemonade.

ELECTION OR "RUM CAKE"

(A favorite of Abraham Lincoln)

1 cup chopped pecans (½ on top, ½ in pan)

1 yellow cake mix with pudding in the mix

2 pkgs. French Vanilla instant pudding mix

½ cup oil

½ cup water

½ cup light rum

4 eggs

Note: Lower oven rack or cake will rise to top of oven. Grease and flour bundt pan. Sprinkle half of chopped nuts in bottom. Reserve other half for glaze instructions. Blend remaining ingredients, except glaze, in a mixer for 2-3 minutes. Pour into pan and bake at 325 degrees for 50 to 60 minutes. Test with straw for doneness. When done, follow glaze instructions while cake is still hot.

Glaze:

1 cup margarine or butter

1/2 cup rum

1 cup sugar

1/4 cup water

Mix, bring to boil and boil for 2 minutes. Poke holes in top of cake with ice pick, pour most of glaze over hot cake, and stand in pan for 30 minutes. Remove cake from pan and pour remaining glaze over top of cake.

PLANTATION ICED TEA

4 cups water

7 small tea bags

12 mint leaves

½ cup sugar

1 (6 oz) can frozen lemonade concentrate

1 (12 oz) can pineapple juice

Ice for serving

Pour 4 cups boiling water over teabags, mint, and sugar in a pitcher. Steep for 30 minutes. Remove tea bags, squeezing out excess liquid. Remove mint. Prepare lemonade according to instructions and add to tea. Add pineapple juice and stir. Serve over ice.

Clockwise from left: *Nighttime on the boards, Yummy Rum Cake, Teapot fountain, Dinner on the Boards with Momma Dean at Meador Homestead ("Y'all c'mon!")*

A Festival of Food

A Menu Honoring Famous Mississippians and Their Favorite Food

Menu

Fried Peanut Butter and Banana Sandwich (Elvis Presley)

Shrimp Eudora (Eudora Welty)

Chili (Brett Favre)

Barbecued Chicken (William Faulkner)

Cheeseburger in Paradise (Jimmy Buffett)

Buttermilk Cornbread (Faith Hill)

Mixed Berries (Oprah Winfrey)

Turnip Greens (Morgan Freeman)

Lemon Iced Box Pie (Tennessee Williams)

Peach Cobbler (William Faulkner)

Southern Mint Iced Tea

Decorations: Set up tables with memorabilia from the famous Mississippians such as pictures of artists, books written by the authors, and a map of Mississippi showing birthplaces. Play music from Buffet, Hill, Presley, and other musicians.

In the late 1800s, artisans would travel the countryside selling their wares. In exchange for a night's stay or a hot meal, they would make or repair a piece of furniture, weave a basket, or paint a picture. The artisan who came to the Meador Homestead cabin must have been given a piece of material and told to paint a picture of something the family had never seen before. Today, a painting of the northeast coast of America hangs above the mantel of the south room. Both artist and family could proudly proclaim the velvet cloth painting as a work of art. These kinds of happenings are still going on at Meador Homestead.

Each year at Meador Homestead, we host the MS ARTeast Festival. This is an old, country-time gathering where we celebrate the arts and honor the artists of the greatest state in the USA—Mississippi. Artists of all genres such as woodturning, glassblowing, painting, photography, pottery, and writing, come from all over the state to the one day event to show off their talent and sell their treasures to be passed on to many generations. Booths are set up, artists proudly smile, customers browse and buy, and a good social interaction is had by all.

A festival with food is even better, and famous Mississippians love to eat as well. To honor those artists who have helped Mississippi distinguish herself from all others, we have included their favorite food for our menu. You can't have a Mississippi meal without Elvis, the King of Rock and Roll, and his Fried Peanut Butter and Banana Sandwich. And who can forget Jimmy Buffett's "Cheeseburger in Paradise?" Writers such as Eudora Welty, Tennessee Williams, and William Faulkner have helped show the world the true South and the heart of America in their works, and we honor them with their special dishes of Shrimp Eudora, Barbecued Chicken, and Lemon Iced Box Pie.

My great-grandfather made his living, besides preaching, by working the family dairy farm on the hill. After milking the cows, putting the clabber into the wooden churn to make butter, and collecting the eggs, he and Ms. Lena would faithfully load the old wagon with their dairy products and make their way down the dusty road to the city homes of Hattiesburg to sell their "art." Throughout the years, the farm also hosted a pecan orchard, grew sugar cane from which they made wonderful molasses, and raised cattle. Like most southeasterners, their farm was self-sufficient.

I'm sure if my great grandfather were living today, he would have proudly set up a booth at the ARTeast festival to sell his products. He would let you drink the excess milk and clabber, skimmed off from the top of the old milk churn. And if you were lucky, he might present you with a tiny beautiful basket he had carved out of a peach seed for a little girl's necklace. Yes, it would prove there is an artist in all of us.

So come to our festival where we celebrate the creative spirit of Mississippians. Enjoy art, architecture, landscape, history, and good food like none other. And if you take the time to stop, you'll meet the greatest Artist of all. He has painted a picture of spectacular cedars and crepe myrtles which change in color from dawn to dusk. We call His painting "A Little Heaven on Earth."

FRIED PEANUT BUTTER AND BANANA SANDWICH

2 slices white bread

2 Tbsp butter

1 small ripe banana

2 Tbsp creamy peanut butter

Place pieces of white bread in a toaster on light setting. Heat skillet over medium heat with butter. While the bread is toasting, in a small bowl, mash the banana with a fork until it reaches a smooth consistency. Using a knife, take both pieces of the toasted bread and spread half the peanut butter on each slice, topping 1 side with the mashed banana. Place 1 slice of bread on top of the other forming a sandwich. Place sandwich in hot skillet browning each side, flipping with a spatula. Take out of skillet, slice on a diagonal, and serve.

Previous page: *How sweet it is! A party honoring Mississippi Artists*
On this page: *The artwork is only half the fun. Food like Elvis's favorite (below) really Rock's the house!*
Top right: *Painting on velvet (c. 1900)*

SHRIMP EUDORA

2 cups milk

2 slices onion

2 sprigs parsley

½ cup butter, divided

4 Tbsp flour

4 Tbsp whipping cream

Salt

¼ tsp white pepper

¼ tsp nutmeg

¼ tsp ginger

6 dashes hot sauce

1 tsp dried green onion

4 cups fresh mushroom

1 ½ lbs medium shrimp, uncooked

1 tsp chopped fresh parsley

2 Tbsp sherry

1 loaf French bread, cut and toasted

Paprika

Scald milk in saucepan with onions and parsley. Strain and set aside. Melt ¼ cup butter in a skillet; add flour, making a paste. Add milk and cook, stirring constantly, until mixture is thickened and bubbly. Stir in whipping cream, salt, pepper, nutmeg, ginger, hot sauce, and green onion. Set aside. Sauté mushrooms in remaining butter in skillet. Peel and devein shrimp. Combine sauce, mushrooms, parsley, and shrimp; cook over low heat until shrimp turn pink (about 5 minutes). Stir in sherry before serving. Serve over toasted bread and sprinkle with paprika. Yield: 6 servings.

CHILI

4 lbs boneless chuck roast, cut into ½ inch pieces

2 Tbsp chili powder

2 (6 oz) cans tomato paste

1 (32 oz) can beef broth

2 (8 oz) cans tomato sauce

2 tsp minced garlic

1 tsp salt

1 tsp oregano

1 tsp ground cumin

1 tsp paprika

1 tsp onion powder

½ tsp ground black pepper

¼ tsp ground red pepper

Tortilla chips and sour cream

Cheese, shredded

Onion, chopped

Brown meat in a Dutch oven. Remove meat. Add chili powder to drippings and cook. Stir in tomato paste and cook for 5 minutes. Return beef to Dutch oven. Stir in beef broth and next 9 ingredients and bring to a boil. Reduce and simmer uncovered, stirring occasionally for 1 ½ hours or until beef is tender. Serve with toppings of chips, sour cream, cheese, and onion.

BARBECUED CHICKEN

1 cup butter

¾ cup lemon juice

2 tsp garlic salt

2 Tbsp paprika

2 tsp dried oregano

4 chickens, halved

3 tsp salt

½ tsp pepper

¾ cup ketchup

4 Tbsp mustard

¾ cup vinegar

½ cup water

2 Tbsp Worcestershire sauce

Melt butter and add lemon juice, garlic salt, paprika, and oregano. Place chickens in large baking dish and sprinkle with salt and pepper. Pour marinade over chickens. Cover and marinate 4 hours or overnight, turning occasionally. Before putting in oven, combine ketchup, mustard, vinegar, water, and Worcestershire sauce and pour over chicken. Cook at 350 degrees for 2 hours or until chicken is tender. Turn chicken frequently. Yield: 12 servings.

CHEESEBURGER IN PARADISE

1 lb ground chuck

Salt

Lemon pepper

Lea & Perrin sauce

American cheese

Toppings of your choice

Season ground chuck with salt, lemon pepper, Lea & Perrin sauce, or seasonings of your choice. Form into the size patties you prefer and fry or grill. Layer with a slice of cheese and then follow the Jimmy Buffet song: "I like mine with lettuce and tomatoes, Heinz 57, and French fried potatoes." Enjoy!

BUTTERMILK CORNBREAD

2 Tbsp vegetable oil or shortening

1 cup yellow or white cornmeal

1 Tbsp all-purpose flour

1 ½ tsp baking powder

¼ tsp baking soda

¼ tsp salt

1 cup buttermilk

1 large egg

Heat oil in an 8-inch cast iron skillet or muffin pans by putting in a 450 degree oven. Remove from oven when hot. Combine cornmeal and next 4 ingredients in a bowl. Stir together buttermilk and egg; add to dry ingredients, stirring just until moistened. Pour into hot skillet. Bake for 20 minutes or until golden. Yield: 6 to 8 servings.

MIXED BERRIES

Place strawberries, blueberries, blackberries, or any berry of choice in a small fruit dish and enjoy!

TURNIP GREENS

This recipe can be found on page 100.

Facing page: *Chicken simmering in the oven & Brett Favre's chili*
On this page: *Crowd pleasers - wood turners & painters*

LEMON ICED BOX PIE

1 box vanilla wafers

2 sticks lightly salted butter

1 cup lemon juice

2 cans condensed milk

2 egg yolks

6 egg whites

½ tsp cream of tartar

½ tsp vanilla extract

¾ cup sugar

In a food processor, finely crush vanilla wafers. Melt butter. Mix melted butter and vanilla wafers into two 9-inch pie plates and shape with fingers. In a large bowl, mix lemon juice, condensed milk, and egg yolks. Pour mixture into pie plates. In another bowl, beat egg whites with cream of tartar, vanilla extract, and sugar until stiff white peaks form. Pour over pie. Bake in oven at 350 degrees to brown meringue (about 20 minutes). Cool to room temperature and put in refrigerator until ice cold.

This page top: *Tennessee Williams' luscious lemon pie*
Middle: *Local actors perform*
Bottom: *Blueberries please the palette.*

Facing page:
Top: *The fruity sweetness of Faulkner's cobbler*
Middle right & bottom left: *Crowd pleasers - Paul Bravo's wooden bowls & Greg Harkins (presidential chair maker)*

PEACH COBBLER

6 medium peaches, peeled and sliced

5 slices white bread, crust removed

1 ½ cups sugar

2 Tbsp flour

1 egg

½ cup butter, melted

Place peaches in an 8-inch square dish coated with Pam. Cut each slice of bread into 5 long strips, and place evenly over fruit. In a bowl, combine sugar, flour, egg, and butter. Pour over fruit and bread. Bake at 350 degrees for 35 minutes.

SOUTHERN MINT ICED TEA FROM SIMPLY TEAVINE TEA ROOM

A Thiskamas Affair

A Holiday Harvest with New Traditions

MENU

Wassail • Cheese Bake Dip • Sausage Balls

Slow-Cooked Chili • Turkey in a Bag

Cornbread Dressing and Gravy

Squash Casserole • Squaw Corn

Asparagus Casserole • Asian Coleslaw

Yellow Cake with Caramel Icing

Mom's Chocolate Nut Clusters

Christmas Delight • Pumpkin Pie

Tea: Emily's Pumpkin Crème

In the year 1884, a man by the name of "Pompey Jones" bought from the US Government the 40 acre parcel of land where Meador Homestead sits today. It didn't take long for the cabin to be filled with life when in 1887, J. T. and Jennie Arnold moved into the two room dog trot cabin with their eight children. Needless to say, it was quite cramped, but the family didn't mind because there was much love amongst them, and that was all that mattered. My step-great-grandmother, Ms. Lena, was one of those eight children, and she had a sister named Agnes. Now Agnes never married, but when she grew up, she moved to Atlanta, Georgia, to be the matriarch of a children's home there. She must have made a lasting impression on many a young one because when she died, the flag at the state capitol building in Atlanta was flown at half mast to honor her legacy. The same feelings for "Aunt Agnes" were felt by the many nieces and nephews back home in Mississippi. She didn't get to come home to the cabin at Christmas time very often, but whatever time of the year she came, it was "Christmas" for all the family, young and old alike. "Christmas" can be any time of the year, as long as family is together sharing traditions of the past and growing a harvest of new ones for generations to come.

One of the greatest joys in life is watching children wake up on Christmas morning. To hear the running of little feet, followed by the laughter and squeals of seeing what Santa brought them is priceless. But children grow up, move away (like Aunt Agnes), marry, and have children of their own. Being together on Christmas morning becomes an elusive dream as new parents jockey to satisfy their in-laws, grandparents, and children. That's why my family has created a new holiday, combining Thanksgiving and Christmas called "Thiskamas." Thiskamas is held on the 1st weekend of December each year, and the entire family gathers at the cabin to spend a few days before the hustle and bustle of shopping, parties, church cantatas, and traveling begins. We combine old traditions of the two holidays, such as sharing blessings at the table with five kernels of corn, opening up "Momma Dean's" handmade stockings to find the ever-faithful one dollar bill in the toe that Santa has left us, and of course, reading from *The Advent Jesse Tree*, a book I wrote over twenty years ago to remember Christ and the true meaning of Christmas. We have even started new traditions such as playing "Dirty Santa," each planting a tree on the land, and enjoying our Iron Skillet Chili cooked over the fire. In the morning the children wake, just like their parents did many years before, and hurry to the north room of the cabin to find the present Santa has brought them on his trial run before he visits the rest of the children of the world on Christmas Eve night.

There have been many "Miracles on Cabin Street." Our first Thiskamas we woke to see the land covered with snow that Santa had brought to south Mississippi. We've seen hoof prints from his deer and sleigh tracks in the field by the pond, and my granddaughter and I truly believe we saw Santa and his sleigh in the sky as he traveled back to the North Pole to get ready for Christmas day. You see, it doesn't matter if Christmas is December or summer. Christmas is anytime loved ones gather and miracles happen. We have included some of the food we enjoy at Thiskamas and hope your family will make them a part of your special holiday time. This year, make memories happen with old and new traditions.

Happy Thiskamas!

SAVING PUMPKIN SEEDS FOR PLANTING

Remove the pulp and seeds from inside the pumpkin. Place this in a colander. Next, place the colander under running water. Pick out the seeds from the pulp. Rinse them in the running water.

There will be more seeds inside the pumpkin than you will ever be able to plant, so once you have a good amount of seeds rinsed, choose the biggest seeds. Plan on saving 3 times more pumpkin seeds than the number of plants you want to grow next year. Larger seeds will have a better chance of germinating. Place the rinsed seeds on a dry paper towel. Make sure they are spaced out, otherwise the seeds will stick to one another. Place in a cool, dry spot for 1 week. Once the seeds are dry, store pumpkin seeds for planting in an envelope.

One of the best places to store your pumpkin seed envelope is in your refrigerator. Put your pumpkin seed envelope in a plastic container. Place several holes in the lid of the container to ensure that condensation does not build up on the inside. Place the container with the seeds inside at the very back of the fridge. After the last frost, take pumpkin seeds out and plant in small hills, 5 or 6 seeds a hill. Enjoy watching your pumpkins grow!

Decorations: Combine Thanksgiving and Christmas decorations. Have pilgrim statues wearing Santa Claus hats. Let Santa Claus' reindeer pull a huge cornucopia filled with presents. Use pumpkins with poinsettias or other seasonal flowers placed in them. Perhaps this year you found the perfect pumpkin for Halloween. We have added our recipe of saving pumpkin seeds and how to store them for planting to ensure that you can enjoy them again next year. Maybe this can be one of your new traditions!

TURKEY IN A BAG

1 young turkey (13 to 15 lbs)

2 Tbsp salt

1 tsp pepper

1 onion, quartered

2 stalks celery, chopped

½ cup vegetable oil

¼ tsp paprika

1 Tbsp flour

Browning bag

Previous page: *Thiskamas - a blending of holidays*

Clockwise from below: *Turkey tradition, Holiday Best-sellers & Beauties, Giving thanks merrily, Thiskamas morning - presents await!*

Remove giblets and neck from turkey and reserve for gravy. Rinse turkey and pat dry. Sprinkle turkey with salt and pepper. Place onion and celery inside cavity of turkey and close. Brush entire bird with oil and sprinkle paprika. Put flour in bag and shake to prevent bursting. Place turkey in bag and tie securely. Cut slits in top of bag. Place turkey breast side up and bake at 325 degrees for 2 ½ hours or until meat thermometer is 180 degrees. Transfer turkey to a serving platter and let stand 15 minutes before carving. Serve with Giblet Gravy below.

Giblet Gravy:

Giblets and neck from turkey

1 tsp salt

1 tsp dried green onion

4 Tbsp margarine

4 Tbsp flour

Turkey broth or 1 (14 oz) can chicken broth

⅓ cup milk

Pepper

2 eggs, boiled and chopped

Place giblets, neck, salt, and green onion in a pan. Add water to cover and simmer 2 hours or until giblets are fork-tender. Drain, reserving broth. Remove meat from neck and chop meat and giblets. Reserve. In a saucepan, melt margarine and add flour. Cook until brown color. Add reserved broth from turkey. Stir until smooth and then add milk and pepper to taste. Stir in giblets, neck meat, and hard-boiled eggs.

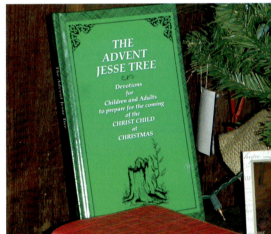

CORNBREAD DRESSING

2 cups self-rising, yellow corn meal

2 cups milk

4 eggs, divided

2 cups chopped celery

1 bunch green onions, finely chopped

1 Tbsp mayonnaise

3-4 Tbsp parsley, chopped

2 Tbsp cooking oil

Crust from one loaf of sandwich bread

2 cans cream of mushroom soup, divided

5-6 cans chicken broth

1 stick butter at room temp

Fresh mushrooms or oysters (opt)

Paprika

Mix corn meal, 1 cup of milk, and 2 eggs. Stir in celery, onion, mayo, and chopped parsley. Warm cooking oil in a pan on top of stove. Transfer the warm oil to your baking dish to cover bottom and sides so that cornbread mixture will not stick. Then pour the rest of the oil in cornbread mixture and mix well. Pour cornbread mixture into this baking dish and cook as you would any cornbread (375 degrees until well-done and brown, usually around 20 minutes). Use a very large mixing bowl to crumble the cooked and cooled cornbread. Add the crust of the sandwich bread, 1 can cream of mushroom soup, and enough chicken broth to saturate mixture (usually a little soupy) and combine well. Work in butter to this mixture. You may also add any other ingredients that you would like, such as fresh mushrooms or oysters. Cover this mixture and let stay in the fridge either overnight or until you are ready to use. (It is better to cook at room temp.) When you are ready to cook, add 2 eggs to mixture and pour mixture into a Pam-sprayed baking dish. Top with paprika and bake at 350 degrees for about 1 hour.

Gravy: Pour 2 cans of chicken broth, 1 can of mushroom soup, and about 4 Tbsp of cooked dressing into a pot. Cook on top of the stove until heated and blended.

ASIAN COLESLAW

½ cup butter

2 (3 oz) pkg of any flavor ramen noodles (discard flavor packets)

½ cup sesame seeds (1 bottle)

½ cup slivered almonds

1 bag coleslaw

4 green onions, chopped

Melt butter in frying pan on medium heat. Break up 2 pkgs of ramen noodles and add to butter. Cook until golden brown. Add sesame seeds and almonds. Drain mixture on paper towels and allow to cool. (This can be done ahead and placed in plastic bag or container, when cooled, until ready for use.) Place bag of coleslaw in a bowl. Chop up 4 green onions and mix. Just before serving, add noodle mixture and dressing (be sure to shake it) to coleslaw and mix.

Dressing:

½ cup olive oil

¾ cup sugar

½ cup vinegar

2 Tbsp soy sauce

Combine all ingredients and shake well. Place in refrigerator and allow to sit for several hours.

Top left: Snow and Thiskamas go together
Right: Bringing the warmth of Thiskamas outside

Evening in December
(Tricia Walker)

As I wait here on this evening in December
I remember how it felt to be a child
This old house still feels the same
all the family will be here in just a while.
I hope Daddy gets here first to build a fire
He's the only one who has that special touch
Then my sister with her kids
And my grandma who I love so very much

Refrain 1: Oh, I'm glad we'll be together on this evening this December
We'll watch the falling snow and hold each other close
I'm so glad we'll be together for an evening to remember
On this night, on this December night.

Sometimes out on the road, it gets so lonely
'Cause I miss those special people I hold dear,
Though our calendars are full
At least for this one night we'll all be here
How the children love this evening in December
And while the smallest ones are playing on the floor
There's a warmth I can't explain
And I feel the love of those who've gone before

Refrain 2:   And I'm glad we're here together on this evening this December
We'll watch the falling snow and hold each other close
I'm so glad we'll be together for an evening to remember
On this night, on this December night.
Keep the fire burning here until we all come back next year
(Repeat Refrain 2)
(Tricia Walker)
Copyright Word Music, Inc.
Big Front Productions, P. O. Box 552, Cleveland, MS 38732, www.bigfrontporch.com

SQUAW CORN

1 onion, chopped

Butter

1 bell pepper, chopped

Corn cut from cob or frozen

Salt and pepper

Sauté onion in butter. Add bell pepper and cook until tender. Add corn and season with salt and pepper.

SLOW-COOKED CHILI

2 lbs ground chuck

2 (15 oz) cans black beans, drained and rinsed

1 (10 oz) can diced tomatoes with green chilies

1 (15 oz) can tomato sauce

1 medium onion, chopped

2 tsp chili powder

1 tsp salt

2 tsp ground cumin

½ tsp black pepper

1 cup thick and chunky salsa

Toppings:
Cheddar cheese, grated

Onions, diced

Sour Cream

Brown meat. In a 6 qt slow cooker, combine meat and all the other ingredients except the salsa and toppings. Cook on preferred setting. Just before serving, stir in salsa. Serve with toppings of choice, such as cheese, diced onions, or sour cream.

ASPARAGUS CASSEROLE

White sauce with cheese (recipe below)

3 hard-boiled eggs, sliced

1 can asparagus

Cracker crumbs

Butter

Make white sauce with cheese. Add eggs, asparagus, and white sauce in two layers into a 1 ½ quart baking dish. Put cracker crumbs on top and dot with butter. Cook at 375 degrees.

White Sauce:
1 cup milk

2 Tbsp flour

2 Tbsp butter

½ tsp salt

½ to 1 cup shredded cheddar

Cheese

Add milk and flour and make paste. Cook on low temperature, stirring constantly. Add butter and salt. Add cheese.

Left: Thiskamas girls & Serving Hearty Chili
Above: The original Thiskamas family (Arnold family)

CHEESE BAKE DIP

½ cup Hellman's mayonnaise

1 (8 oz) pkg cream cheese

2 cups grated cheddar cheese

2 green onions, chopped

6 Ritz crackers, crushed

8 slices bacon, cooked and crumbled

Capt Rodney's Glaze

Crackers

Mix mayo, cream cheese, cheddar, and onions in mixing bowl. Place mixture into greased 9-inch pie pan. Top with crushed crackers and bake at 350 degrees for 15 minutes. Top with bacon and Capt Rodney's Glaze, covering the entire dip. Serve with crackers.

SQUASH CASSEROLE

This recipe can be found on page 27.

SAUSAGE BALLS

1 lb uncooked hot sausage

10 oz sharp cheese, grated

3 cups Bisquick

In a large bowl, mix all three ingredients until it adheres in a large ball. Roll into walnut-size balls. Bake at 375 degrees for 15-20 minutes. Balls will not change size during baking.

Below: Aunt Agnes & Sisters
Bottom: Planting Memories
Right: Pumpkin Pie - A simple dish of gratitude

CHRISTMAS DELIGHT

½ gal pineapple sherbet

½ gal lime sherbet

1 (10 oz) pkg frozen strawberries

Nuts chopped

Cut sherbets into pieces and put in layers in a glass punch bowl. Put half of the strawberries in, then layer again with sherbets. Finish with strawberries and sprinkle nuts on top. Let melt until soft and spoon into sherbet glasses.

YELLOW CAKE WITH CARAMEL ICING

2 cups sugar

2 sticks butter or margarine

4 eggs, separated

2 ⅔ cups Swans Down cake flour

4 tsp baking powder

1 cup milk

1 tsp vanilla

Cream sugar and butter until creamy, and then add egg yolks one at a time. Sift flour and baking powder. Add flour gradually, alternating with milk and vanilla. Beat egg whites and fold into mixture. Place in 3 greased and floured 9-inch pans. Bake at 350 degrees for 20 minutes or until done.

Original Caramel Icing (from Aline Darby)

½ cup brown sugar

3 cups granulated sugar

1 cup milk

1 stick margarine

1 box powdered sugar

Put ½ cup brown sugar in thick pan and melt until a liquid. Do not burn. In a separate pan, put rest of sugar and milk on stove and start cooking. Then, add melted brown sugar and cook until soft ball stage. (Soft ball means to drop about a tsp of mixture in a cup of cold water and it will form a soft ball.) When ready, remove from heat. Drop the margarine in pan of sugar and let cool. Then, start beating and slowly add a box of powdered sugar until it gets to the consistency that will hold up while putting being put on a cake.

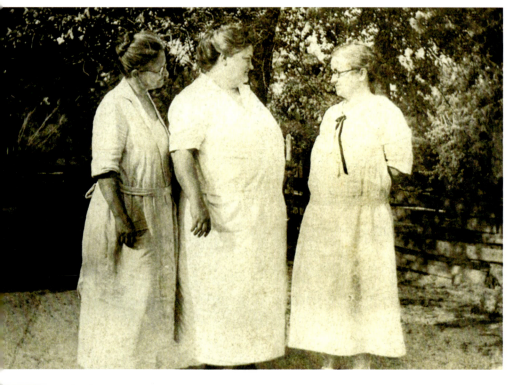

WASSAIL

1 qt hot black tea

1 cup sugar

1 (32 oz) bottle cranberry juice

1 (32 oz) bottle apple juice

2 cups orange juice

¾ cup lemon juice

2 sticks cinnamon

24 whole cloves, divided

Orange slices

Combine hot tea and sugar in a large pot; stir in juices. Add cinnamon and cloves. Boil over medium heat until hot. Garnish with orange slices studded with the rest of the cloves. Yield: 1 gallon.

EMILY'S PUMPKIN CRÈME TEA FROM SIMPLY TEAVINE TEA ROOM

CHOCOLATE NUT CLUSTERS

1 (24 oz) Almond Bark chocolate, chopped

1 (16 oz) jar salted, dry-roasted peanuts

Pretzels or almonds (opt)

Melt bark in microwave for 90 seconds, then intervals of 15 seconds, if needed. Stir in peanuts. Spoon mixture onto waxed paper in small mounds. Let cool and store clusters in airtight container. You could use pretzels or almonds instead of peanuts. Yield: 36 pieces.

PUMPKIN PIE

2 eggs

1 cup sugar

1 tsp cinnamon

½ tsp ginger

1 Tbsp vanilla

1 cup pumpkin

Pinch of salt

1 cup milk

1 (9 in) pie shell

Beat eggs, and then add other ingredients. Put in 9-inch pie shell. Bake for 30 minutes at 375 degrees.

Winter

A New Beginnings Luncheon Tea
A Welcoming Tea for Any Occasion

A Circuit Rider's Tea
A Soup and Sandwich Meal for Those on the Go

Fireside Candlelight Dinner
A Romantic Evening for Two

Cast Iron Cooking
Cabin Comfort Food

Christmas at the Cabin
Comfort and Joy

A New Beginnings Luncheon Tea

A Welcoming Tea for Any Occasion

Menu

Cornbread • Copper Pennies

Sweet Potato Biscuits and Sweet Potato Fries

Champagne Punch • Corned Beef and Cabbage

Collards, Spinach, or Turnip Greens • Broiled Shrimp

"Apple a Day" Pork Chops • Mandarin Oranges and Grapes

Smoky Blue Cheese Cabbage Slaw • Hoppin' John

New Year's Day Soup • Lady Baltimore Cake

Chocolate Round Pound Cake • Peach Crisp

When restoration of the Meador Homestead cabin began in 2009, layer upon layer was removed from the walls in a home that had been loved and lived in for 125 years. The first to come down was the blue sheetrock that I had known for 50 plus years and then came wallpaper after wallpaper, until finally, the 1884 heart pine logs were revealed in all its past glory. As I peeled off strips of the four faded, yet beautiful designs, I wondered when each had first appeared to adorn these hallowed walls. My imagination led to only one sure conclusion. It was every time a new woman came into the house to make it her home.

First, there were the thick trees of 1884, stacked atop each other with the honey-colored chinking between. Then Jennie Arnold arrived with her army of children and attacked the fortress with its first wallpaper in 1887. I'm sure there was much lengthy discussion in 1913 between Ms. Lena and the two mothers living there about how to bring the cabin into the twentieth century with new designs of the time. In 1928, additional wallpaper was layered on as my Grandmother Dean's entrepreneurial spirit filled the place for her husband and two boys. Finally, 1953 came with the newest vogue for sheetrock and wood paneling. It was Jessie Meador, my step-grandmother, who spent hours upon hours staining any exposed wood that had somehow earlier escaped the eyes of the women living there.

When all the additions and changes had been completed, I'm sure there were many invites to "hop in" and stay for supper. The woman could show off her newly-renovated home with blessings from friends for love, health, and prosperity to abound—that is until the next woman would come, bringing her hopes and personality to the walls of the beloved Meador Homestead cabin.

In the South, we celebrate events with certain food. Eager to get off to the best possible start, we will "eat for luck, happiness, and prosperity." And so, our menu brings these traditions to the table to insure success for any "new" occasion. Champagne is used to toast a couple's beginning at wedding receptions, and it is the favorite bubbly to drink as midnight strikes to welcome in the New Year. Our Champagne Punch brings the sparkle to these festive events. Shrimp represents a "long life," and this informal fare served with a toast begins the meal. Our soup certainly has all the good luck ingredients you need with peas and greens. Packed with vitamins, it is sure to help you stay healthy.

Eating greens brings "wealth," and the favorites of Southerners are collard and turnip greens, spinach, and cabbage. Our cabbage slaw gives a modern twist for "bringing in the money." Ham or pork tastes great tucked inside the sweet potato biscuit to be used as an appetizer or with the meal. Pork and apples are a classic combination—and with pork representing "progress" or living "high on the hog," and "health" promised in the old saying, "An apple a day keeps the doctor away," these pork chops are sure to be a hit! Add a sprig of parsley to decorate the dish and "ward off the evil spirits," and be sure to save 12 raisins from the recipe to eat for luck in the months ahead. The Corned Beef and Cabbage brings health, wealth, and happiness all rolled into one dish, and the Copper Pennies, as a salad or side dish, ensure "good eyesight and prosperity" for the future.

Our most colorful dish, rich in history and nutrients, is our Hoppin' John. One legend traces the dish back to the Civil War, when the town of Vicksburg, Mississippi, ran out of food while under attack. The residents and soldiers still had the field-picked legumes, however, and thereafter, the black-eyed pea was considered "lucky." My great-great-grandfather fought in the siege of Vicksburg, so the story is very appropriate for the cabin, along with the "open-house invites" to family and friends. The Lady Baltimore Cake recipe first appeared in a 1906 newspaper article and has been passed down through Southern families ever since. The specialty cake became the favorite wedding cake of the early 1900's, and the nuts, figs, and raisins included in the cake represent "happiness and fertility" to the new couple. This could have been the wedding reception cake served in the north room when couples were married by my great-grandfather on the steps of the cabin. The Chocolate Pound cake baked in a ring shaped circle symbolizes "everlasting life." We complete the meal with our Peach Crisp, representing "love and health."

This menu can be served for a meet-the-new-neighbors party, a meal for the blessing of a new home, a dinner toast to the newlyweds, and, of course, a celebratory event to welcome in the New Year. Whatever the occasion, it is your way of saying, "Hop in, John, and stay for supper!" Our celebration meal ends with an early 1900 blessing that can be used for any new beginning:

"May your heart never empty, may your wallet be full,
Good friends will surround you, may God bless us all,
Keep our health good, and our faith nice and strong,
May our labors be fruitful all the year long."

BUTTERMILK CORNBREAD

This recipe can be found on page 100.

Decorations: Spotless linen, shining crystal, gold glittering ornaments, and a few loose clusters of rosebuds, typical of a budding romance or a new year, impart a charm and suggest the graceful idea of beginning for any welcoming occasion.

Previous page: A New Year's spread
Facing page: Health, wealth, and good fortune - all on one plate!
Right: Corn bread at its best (made in mold) - lathered in butter

COPPER PENNIES

1 lb carrots, sliced and cooked

1 onion, chopped

1 green pepper, diced

1 can tomato soup, undiluted

¼ cup salad oil

¼ cup vinegar

¾ cup sugar

1 tsp Worcestershire sauce

1 tsp prepared mustard

Dash hot pepper sauce

Salt

Pepper

Prepare vegetables. In separate bowl, mix soup, oil, vinegar, sugar, and seasonings. Pour over vegetables and let stand in refrigerator overnight. Serve cold as a salad or as a hot vegetable. Yield: 8 servings.

SWEET POTATO BISCUITS

⅓ cup cold butter or margarine

2 ½ cups biscuit mix

1 cup canned, mashed sweet potato

½ cup milk

Preheat oven to 450 degrees. Cut butter into biscuit mix with a pastry blender until mixture is crumbly. Combine sweet potato and milk and add to biscuit mix. Stir until blended. Turn dough out onto a lightly floured surface and knead. Roll dough to ¾ inch thickness and cut with a round biscuit cutter. Place biscuits on a large, ungreased baking sheet and bake for 10 minutes or until golden. Yield: 22 biscuits.

SWEET POTATO FRIES

1 ½ pounds sweet potatoes

Hot oil

2 Tbsp crushed rosemary (opt)

Salt

Tomato ketchup

Wash sweet potatoes and cut into long thin strips, about ¼ inches thick. Place in ice water for about 15 minutes. Preheat deep fryer. Remove sweet potato fries from water and pat dry with paper towels. Place in hot oil for about 4 minutes or until golden brown. Remove from oil and allow potatoes to drain on paper towels. Sprinkle rosemary and salt over top. Serve with tomato ketchup.

CHAMPAGNE PUNCH

1 cup sugar

1 cup water

1 cup apricot nectar

½ cup lemon juice

1 (64 oz) bottle apple juice

½ (6 oz) can frozen orange juice concentrate, thawed

1 bottle champagne, chilled

1 (12 oz) can ginger ale, chilled

Combine sugar and water in a large pot; bring to a boil, stirring until sugar dissolves. Set aside, and cool. Add apricot nectar and next 3 ingredients to sugar mixture and stir. Pour mixture into a container that will freeze. Freeze for 8 hours. Remove container from freezer, and let stand at room temperature for 30 minutes. Place block in a punch bowl. Add bottle of champagne and ginger ale, stirring gently. Yield: 16 cups.

BEFORE

Left: *My favorite greens*
Far left: *Day lillies welcome the day, A toast to New Bginnings, A gardenia offers a sweet scent, The bride and groom (Dean & Eddie) 40 years before their New Beginnings together*
Bottom: *Breathing new life into the Meador Homestead*

TURNIP GREENS

6 bunches turnip greens

4 slices bacon

2 Tbsp sugar

½ tsp salt

½ tsp pepper

½ cup water

Strip the leaves from the stems. Immerse leaves in water. In an iron skillet, fry bacon over low heat for about 7 minutes. Carefully lift greens from the water and add to the skillet. Turn several times. Add sugar, seasonings, and water. Simmer over very low heat for 3 hours. Remove from liquid and serve hot. Serves 6. (can substitute your favorite Collards or Spinach for Recipe)

CORNED BEEF AND CABBAGE

1 (4 lb) round of corned beef

Onions

Potatoes

Carrots

Cabbage

Mustard

Wash beef and put in Dutch oven to cook on stove. Cover with water. Boil an hour per pound and then turn down to low. An hour before meat is calculated to be done, put in onions and potatoes you desire; 15 minutes later, put in carrots and cabbage. Take roast out and let sit for about 15 minutes before serving. Serve with mustard.

131

Below & Left: *Unearthing the treasure of Meador Homestead*

BROILED SHRIMP

2 pounds large fresh shrimp, unpeeled

½ cup vegetable oil

¼ cup soy sauce

3 Tbsp chopped fresh parsley

1 Tbsp lemon juice

2 garlic cloves, minced

Slices of French bread, toasted

Peel shrimp, leaving tails intact. Place shrimp in a large, shallow broiler pan. Combine oil and next 4 ingredients, and pour over shrimp. Cover and marinate in refrigerator 2 hours. Uncover and broil for 7 to 8 minutes or until shrimp turn pink, stirring once. Serve immediately over French bread. Yield: 4-6 servings.

Below: Bringing good food and fortune to our "new" cabin
Bottom Left: Vintage gold bracelet serves as napkin ring (c.1900)

"APPLE A DAY" PORK CHOPS

6 boneless pork chops	1 apple, peeled and chopped
1 Tbsp fresh or dried rosemary	1 cup raisins or currants
½ tsp salt	2 tsp olive oil
½ tsp pepper	¾ cup apple cider
1 Tbsp rum (opt)	Rosemary sprigs and apple slices

Coat both sides of pork chops evenly with cooking spray. Combine rosemary, salt, pepper and rum. Spread mixture evenly on both sides of pork. Set aside. Cook apple and raisins in hot oil in a large skillet, stirring often for 5 minutes. Add ¼ cup cider, stirring until most of liquid is evaporated. Add remaining cider, and cook 15 minutes or until mixture is thickened. Cook pork chops in a large skillet coated with cooking spray 5 minutes on each side or until done. Top with apple mixture. Garnish with rosemary and apple slices. Yield: 6 servings.

MANDARIN ORANGES AND GRAPES

Mandarin oranges

Grapes

Mandarin oranges are a Chinese symbol for good fortune. In some countries, eating 12 grapes for the months of the New Year will ensure prosperity. Have oranges and grapes ready to eat as a snack or for your meal.

SMOKY BLUE CHEESE CABBAGE SLAW

1 small head cabbage, cut into 8 wedges

2 carrots

4 scallons

¼ cup crumbled blue cheese

Dressing:

½ cup mayonnaise

½ cup sour cream

2 tbsp apple cider vinegar

2 tbsp sugar

Salt and pepper to taste

Cabbage Slaw: Cut cabbage into wedges and smoke. (I used a cold smoker for 4 hours.) Place in bowl and seal tightly. Refrigerate overnight. Thinly slice cabbage and place in large bowl. Peel and shred carrots, and thinly slice the scallions. Toss together with the blue cheese.

Dressing: In a small bowl, whisk together mayonnaise, sour cream, vinegar, sugar, salt, and pepper. Pour over the cabbage mixture and toss well. Yield: 6 to 8 servings.

HOPPIN' JOHN

3 bacon slices or cooked ham hocks, chopped	undrained	Red pepper flakes, crushed (opt)
½ onion, chopped	1 cup uncooked long-grain rice	Tomatoes, chopped (opt)
1 cup water	½ tsp thyme	Shredded cheddar cheese (opt)
1 (15 oz) can black-eyed peas,	Salt and pepper to taste	

Cook bacon until crisp and add onion, stirring constantly. Stir in water and peas; bring to a boil. Cover, reduce heat and stir in rice and seasonings. Cook until rice is tender (about 20 to 25 minutes). You may add tomatoes if desired. Put in serving dish and sprinkle shredded cheese over top. Yield: 2 to 4 servings.

NEW YEAR'S DAY SOUP

Olive oil

1 cup diced ham

2 stalks celery, chopped

1 onion, chopped

2 carrots, chopped

2 garlic cloves, minced

2 (15 oz) cans black-eyed peas, undrained

2 (14 ½ oz) cans chicken broth

2 (14 ½ oz) cans stewed tomatoes, undrained

1 (14 ½ oz) can diced tomatoes, undrained

1 (8 oz) can tomato sauce

1 ½ cups fresh spinach, chopped

½ cup fresh parsley, chopped

½ tsp pepper

Fresh spinach for garnish, chopped

Sauté first 5 ingredients in olive oil in a Dutch oven until vegetables are tender. Stir in peas and next 4 ingredients and bring to a boil. Cover, reduce heat, and simmer 1 hour. Stir in spinach, parsley, and pepper. Garnish with fresh chopped spinach. Yield: 10 cups.

Above, Left and Below: Celebrating new beginnings of all kinds

LADY BALTIMORE CAKE

6 egg whites

2 cups sugar

1 cup butter

1 cup milk

3 ½ cups flour

2 tsp baking powder

Frosting:
3 cups sugar

½ cup water

½ cup butter

2 egg whites

1 cup raisins

1 cup nuts

1 cup figs

Lightly beat the whites of six eggs with ¼ cup sugar and reserve. In a separate bowl, cream butter and remaining sugar. Add milk, flour, and baking powder, adding reserved eggs last of all. Bake in two 9-inch buttered pans at 350 degrees for 15 to 20 minutes. For the frosting, boil sugar and water for 5 minutes until it threads and is stringy. Beat the whites of two eggs very lightly and pour the boiling sugar slowly into it, mixing well. Take out of this mixture enough for the top and sides of the cake. Add fruit and nuts to the remainder for the filling between the two layers.

CHOCOLATE ROUND POUND CAKE

½ lb butter (2 sticks)

½ cup shortening

3 cups sugar

5 eggs

1 Tbsp vanilla

½ tsp baking powder

½ tsp salt

4 Tbsp cocoa

3 cups flour

1 cup milk

Cream butter and shortening; add sugar, eggs, and vanilla. Cream well. Sift dry ingredients together. Add alternately with milk, starting and ending with flour. Bake at 325 degrees for 1 hour 20 minutes. Do not open oven during baking period. Use greased and floured tube or bundt pan.

PEACH CRISP

4 cups sliced fresh or frozen peaches

¾ cup sugar, divided

½ tsp ground cinnamon

1 cup all-purpose flour

½ cup butter

Toss peaches, ¼ cup sugar, and cinnamon in a large bowl; spoon into a lightly greased baking dish and set aside. Combine flour and remaining sugar; cut in butter with a pastry blender until mixture is crumbly. Sprinkle on top of peaches. Bake at 350 degrees for 35 to 40 minutes. Yield: 6 to 8 servings.

Clockwise from left: Looking for more treasure in the 1885 barn, Meador Homestead, Favorite wedding cake of the early 1900's, A blessing for the new year, Preserving future beginnings

A Circuit Rider's Tea

A Soup and Sandwich Meal for Those on the Go

MENU

Winter Apple Salad

Potato and Corn Chowder

Turkey, Bacon, and Muenster Sandwich

Preacher Man's Stew

Grilled Apple and Cheese Sandwich

Hoecakes • Hummingbird Cake

Heavenly Hash Cake

Coffee, Tea, or Root Beer (Our "Sassafras" Tea)

Decorations: Use grape vines for napkin rings and as a runner with flowers and foliage interspersed in them. Display horse figurines, old Bibles and songbooks, eyeglasses, or antique bells to carry the theme of the circuit rider on the go. Wooden or metal chargers with old mugs and silverware will give the table rustic charm. You might even want to tie a Bible verse to each tea cup to warm the soul!

My great-great-grandfather was a part of a group of clergy in the Methodist church who were assigned to travel around specific geographic territories to minister to settlers and organize congregations. These dedicated men in the 1800s would serve more than one congregation at a time and travel on horseback from one rural area to the next, thus giving them the name of "circuit riders." This calling was taken very seriously as seen in Levi Parks Meador's license to preach that was found in an old metal box at the cabin:

"This certifies that Levi P. Meador, having applied to us, after being recommended by his church, for license to preach the gospel in the Methodist Episcopal Church South, after due inquiry concerning his gifts, grace, and usefulness we think him a suitable person to preach, and we accordingly grant him license. Signed by order of the Quarterly Conference for Hillsborough circuit, This 19 day of Sept. 1861."

And so with saddlebag filled with his Bible, shaped note songbook, and bell to ring, "Levi Pa" would mount his faithful horse "Old Jim" and ride off to tiny, remote v,illages and farms scattered throughout the area where he was appointed to preach salvation to all. Sometimes it would take weeks to make the circuit, staying in homes of whomever would host him until he would be on his way to another church community or village for more evangelizing and the giving of the sacraments. Levi Pa's circuit riding days were interrupted by the Civil War, but he still faithfully continued preaching the gospel to the soldiers by serving as a chaplain at the Siege of Vicksburg. After the war, he continued to serve by moving from church to church regularly as appointments were made for only one year by the Methodist church.

My great-grandfather Walton Price Meador served in the same way. Mounting his horse "Old John," Grand Pap would ride year-round, often times crossing rivers and creeks in ice-cold water to conduct worship and visit members of his charge, whether it be in other log cabins, fields, or several churches. He would travel with few possessions—carrying only what he could carry on horseback. After making a circuit, he would return home for a few days, get some rest and a few hot meals, and then go back on his horse to go again. As you can see, Methodist circuit riders were always on the move!

The Circuit Rider's Tea is as close as we'll ever get to a fast food restaurant menu. This food can be cooked ahead, warmed up, and ready to eat within minutes to leave precious time to sit around the table and be with family and friends. It is quick, and simple, and will warm the tummy as well as the soul!

Both the Potato and Corn Chowder and Preacher Man's Soup are hearty and perfect for any weather. Equally satisfying is our turkey sandwich, loaded into a sourdough or roasted garlic bread loaf with bacon, Muenster cheese, and a tangy vinaigrette sauce. Everyone loves a grilled cheese sandwich, and we have created a fabulous flavor teaser, filled with cheese and complemented with apples and olives.

The term "hoecake" was used by the field hands in the South to describe the pancake biscuit. The bread was always baked on a hoe on hot coals in front of a wood fire, hence the name hoecakes. When Grand Pap came home, he would have most assuredly sopped up the sugar cane syrup made from the land with these biscuits, followed by a gulping down of some good hot coffee or sassafras tea made from the sassafras tree in the yard. Fast food couldn't be so good!

Previous page: Methodist Circuit Riders Levi P. Meador (bottom left) and W.P. Meador on their faithful horses "Old Jim" and "Old John"
Above: Winter Apple Salad   Top: Grand Pap with Bible,

WINTER APPLE SALAD

1 (20 oz) can crushed pineapple, undrained

⅔ cup sugar

1 (3 oz) pkg lemon jello

1 (8 oz) pkg cream cheese, softened

1 cup diced, unpeeled apples

½ to 1 cup chopped nuts

1 cup diced celery

1 cup whipped topping

Combine pineapple and sugar in saucepan. Boil 3 minutes. Add jello and cream cheese. Combine until smooth. Cool. Fold in apples, nuts, celery, and whipped topping. Pour into 9 x 13 pan and refrigerate. Keep cool.

POTATO AND CORN CHOWDER

5 slices bacon

1 onion, thinly sliced and separated into rings

2 medium potatoes, peeled and diced

½ cup water

1 (17 oz) can cream-style corn

2 cups milk

1 tsp salt

Pepper to taste

In large pan, cook bacon until crisp. Remove, crumble, and set aside. Reserve 3 tsp bacon drippings in pan; discard remainder. Add onion rings and cook until lightly browned. Add diced potatoes and water; cook over medium heat until potatoes are tender (15 to 20 minutes). Add corn, milk, salt, and pepper. Cook until heated. Pour into warmed bowls; top each serving with crumbled bacon.

TURKEY, BACON, AND MUENSTER SANDWICH

4 bacon slices, fully cooked

1 loaf sourdough or roasted garlic bread

¼ cup balsamic vinaigrette

½ lb thinly sliced, smoked deli turkey

1 (12 oz) jar roasted red bell peppers, drained and sliced

1 oz slices Muenster or Havarti cheese

Cook bacon. Cut tops off bread loaf and reserve; hollow out loaf, leaving a 1 inch thick shell. Drizzle 2 Tbsp vinaigrette evenly in bottom of bread shell. Layer with half of turkey, peppers, and cheese. Repeat layers and top with bacon. Drizzle evenly with remaining 2 Tbsp of vinaigrette and cover with reserved bread top. Press down firmly and wrap in plastic wrap. Chill at least 1 hour or up to 8 hours before serving. Cut to make 4 sandwiches.

Above: *Circuit bell and songbook passed down from father to son,*
Top & bottom: *Comfort Chowder & Hearty Sandwich - Perfect for a weary traveler*

PREACHER MAN'S STEW

2 Tbsp olive oil

4 boneless, skinless chicken breasts, cut into bite size pieces

1 cup chopped onion

1 small green bell pepper, chopped

1 small yellow bell pepper, chopped

1 tsp chopped garlic

1 (14 ½ oz) can stewed tomatoes

1 (15 oz) can pinto beans, drained

¾ cup medium picante sauce

1 Tbsp chili powder

1 Tbsp ground cumin

Shredded cheddar cheese and sour cream

In large pot or Dutch oven, heat olive oil. Add chicken, onion, bell peppers, and garlic, cooking until chicken is done. Add tomatoes, beans, picante sauce, chili powder, and cumin. Reduce heat to low and simmer 25 minutes or up to 2 hours. Place in bowls and top with cheese and sour cream. Yield: 6 servings.

GRILLED APPLE AND CHEESE SANDWICH

1 cup shredded sharp cheddar cheese

1 cup finely chopped cooking apple

½ cup minced pimento-stuffed olives

¼ cup mayonnaise

8 slices whole wheat bread

Melted butter

Combine cheese, apple, olives, and mayonnaise in a medium bowl and stir well. Spread cheese mixture evenly on one side of 4 slices of bread. Top with remaining bread slices and brush with melted butter. Put on hot griddle, buttered side down. Butter top slice. Cook, turning sandwiches until golden brown. Yield: 4 sandwiches.

HOECAKES

2 cups flour

1 cup milk

1 tsp yeast

2 Tbsp butter, softened

Optional toppings:
Fruit or fruit preserves

Molasses or cane syrup

Mix ingredients well and knead. Roll out with rolling pin, cut crisscross, like diamonds, with a knife. Cook on a griddle (like pancakes) and serve with butter, fruit, and molasses/cane syrup.

HUMMINGBIRD CAKE

3 cups all-purpose flour

2 cups sugar

1 tsp salt

1 tsp soda

1 tsp cinnamon

3 eggs, beaten

1 ½ cup salad oil

1 ½ tsp vanilla

1 (8 oz) can crushed pineapple, undrained

2 cups chopped pecans or walnuts

2 cups chopped bananas

Combine dry ingredients in a large mixing bowl; add eggs and salad oil, stirring until dry ingredients are moistened. Do not beat. Stir in vanilla, pineapple, 1 cup pecans, and bananas. Spoon the batter into 3 well-greased and floured 9-inch cake pans. Bake at 350 degrees for 25 to 30 minutes or until done. Cool in pans 10 minutes; remove from pans and cool completely. Spread frosting between layers and on top and sides of cake. Sprinkle with 1 cup chopped pecans.

Cream Cheese Frosting:

1 (8 oz) pkg softened cream cheese

½ cup softened butter or margarine

1 (16 oz) pkg powdered sugar

1 tsp vanilla

Combine cream cheese and butter in large mixing bowl; cream until smooth. Add powdered sugar, beating until light and fluffy. Stir in vanilla.

Clockwise from left: *From sandwich to dessert - so much to eat and so little time*

HEAVENLY HASH CAKE

2 cups sugar

1 ½ cups plain flour

4 Tbsp cocoa

2 tsp baking powder

2 sticks margarine, melted

4 whole eggs, slightly beaten

1 cup chopped pecans

2 tsp vanilla

1 (12 oz) pkg miniature marshmallows

Frosting:
1 stick margarine

4 Tbsp cocoa

6 Tbsp evaporated milk

1 (16 oz) box powdered sugar

Mix dry ingredients. Stir margarine into eggs, and then mix into dry ingredients. Do not beat. Add nuts and vanilla. Bake in lightly greased and floured 9 x 13 inch pan at 400 degrees for approximately 15 minutes. You must test for doneness according to oven. After removing from oven, pour marshmallows over cake. For frosting, start about 5 minutes before cake is done. Melt margarine. Add cocoa and evaporated milk; bring to a boil. Pour over sugar and beat to remove lumps. Pour over marshmallows on cake. (The icing will spread better if a little more evaporated milk is added.)

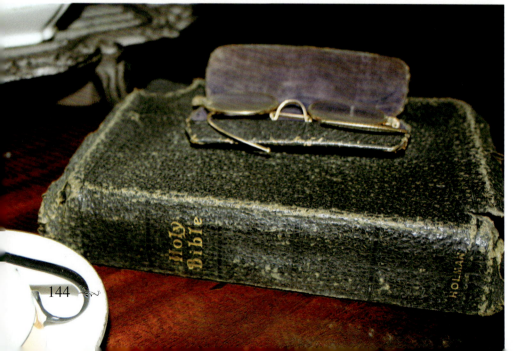

Top: *Experience Heaven with this Cake*
Middle: *A simple respite from the road*
Bottom: *Glasses c. 1900 with Grandfather's Bible*

Above: *The legacy lives on! 6th-generation "Chuck" Meador ordained as a Methodist Preacher in the Mississippi conference*
Right: *Levi P. Meador's license to preach (1861)* Below: *A circuit rider's path*

*If it pleases you, stop here for awhile.
Rest as my servants prepare food to
refresh you. Stay awhile
before continuing on your journey.
Genesis 18 : 4-5*

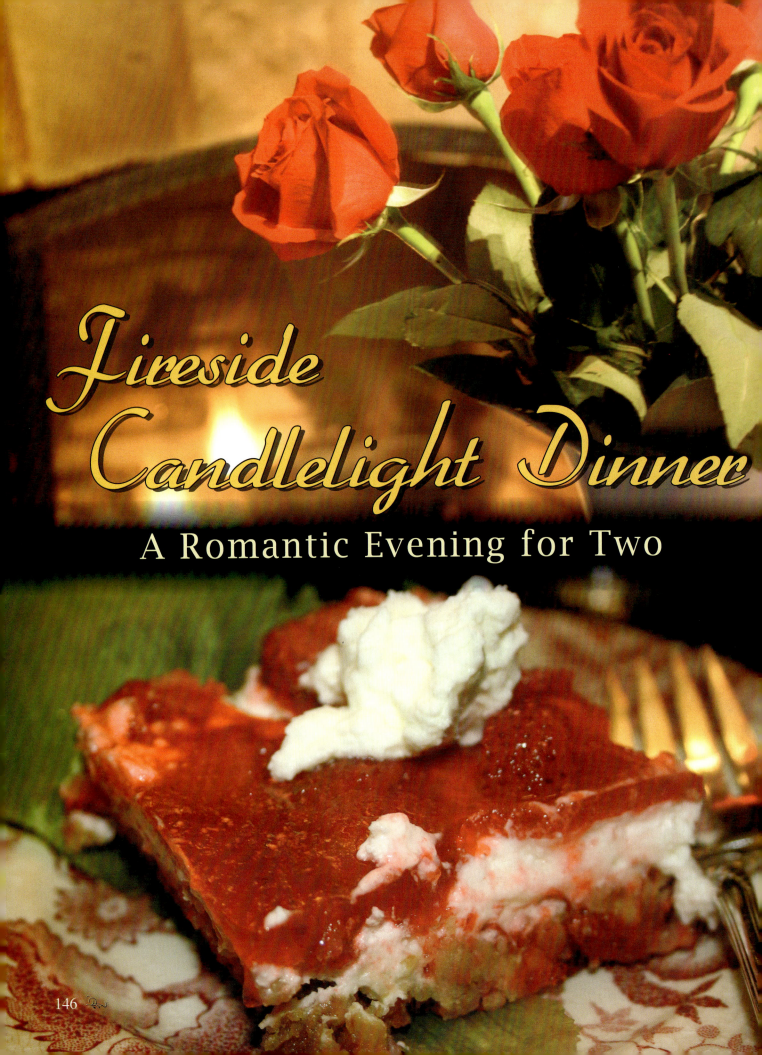

Fireside Candlelight Dinner
A Romantic Evening for Two

MENU

Nancy's Cheese Ring

Strawberry Congealed Salad

Beef and Vegetable Stew

Steamed Broccoli

Herbed Crescent Rolls

$100 Fudge Pie

Decadent Cherries

Romeo and Juliet Heart-Shaped Hot Tea

Decorations: Set up a table for two in front of the fire using your finest china, linens, and silverware. Add roses, scattering a few petals on the table, a card, and music to make a romantic atmosphere. The heart-shaped tea can be ordered from Simply TeaVine (Hattiesburg, MS).

We have discovered a powerful entity that never fails to work its therapeutic magic. It releases all of our senses to experience. It is sitting in front of a fire.

The fireplaces at Meador Homestead are the centerpiece of each room. It is at the fireside where family and friends gather for warm conversation and thought. There will be laughter and song, perhaps even tears, and stories told of those who came before us. Sitting in front of a fire permits one to become transformed, as if the world outside that gentle glow of light does not exist. One is allowed to probe distant depths of his or her mind that are seldom explored. Those varying hues of orange, blue, and yellow jump and flicker as if in an orchestrated dance of fairies. A fire is mesmerizing, hearts are warmed, and the sound of the hiss and crackle brings healing.

With no central air or heat, it was by the fireside the family sat in earlier times to read, cook, or contemplate. Once, my grandfather came in to see my great-great-grandmother sitting in her tiny rocking chair close to a very small fire. He asked her why she didn't build a bigger fire to which she replied, "White men build a big fire and have to stand far away. Better to be like the Indians and sit close to a small fire. It's not wasteful." Her words are profound, for the warmth of the fire calls us to come closer into a place of stillness and serenity. Time stands quiet as we bask in its warm glow.

The smell is unmistakable. Guests at the cabin will walk in and immediately be transported to a time when as children they visited their grandparents' home or as teenagers, they sat and sang "Kum Ba Yah" around a campfire. Whatever the memory, it is pleasant. The modern world may tell us to avoid such odors as those emitted by a fireplace. Yet, the smell means comfort and safety to us, and we are drawn to it.

And who can forget the unforgettable taste of chestnuts roasted on an open fire, toasty marshmallows, or beef stew simmered in the old Dutch oven? Indeed, a fire satisfies all the senses!

Our menu consists of food that can be prepared ahead of time, so the cook can enjoy the special dinner, also. Each dish will hold several days in the refrigerator. We start off with my sister's wonderful cheese dip, followed by my grandmother's Strawberry congealed salad, a favorite of guests who eat at the cabin. I chose my Beef and

Vegetable Stew, which reminds me of Julia Child's Beef Bourguignon, but it is a lot easier to make. You can place the stew atop rice or noodles for a complete meal. Men and women love the Crescent rolls with an herb twist, and we have added steamed broccoli as the side. Finally, we give chocolate lovers a treat with our Fudge pie and Decadent Cherries. Thirty five years ago, a lady paid $100 for the pie recipe. Can you imagine what it would cost now? Our Decadent cherries are just that—decadent. Soaked in Southern Comfort, one of these indulgent cherries gives a "wow" to the ending of a perfect fireside dinner. You can serve it separately or place it on top of whipped cream on the fudge pie.

There is nothing more romantic than setting a small table for two in front of a crackling fire to fan the flames of love. Add candlelight, music, and good food, and let the world go by!

"Let us linger here by the fire, for I am warmed by your company, and this mystery of love."

NANCY'S CHEESE RING

2 cups grated sharp cheddar cheese

2 cups mild cheddar cheese, grated

1 bunch green onions, finely chopped

1 ¾ cup mayonnaise

Red pepper, crushed, to taste

1 cup chopped pecans

1 jar strawberry preserves

Crackers of your choice

Mix cheese, onions, mayo, pepper, and pecans. Pour into dish or mold. Serve with strawberry preserves and crackers.

Previous page: *Exciting the senses*
Clockwise from far right: *Food for the soul, Words of Love, Postcard found in the cabin (has anything changed?), Table by the fire invites romance*

STRAWBERRY CONGEALED SALAD

3 Tbsp powdered sugar

¾ margarine, melted

2 cups crushed pretzels

1 (3 oz) pkg cream cheese

¾ cup sugar

1 (4 oz) tub Cool Whip

1 (6 oz) box strawberry Jello

2 cups boiling water

1 (16 oz) container frozen strawberries

For 1st layer, cream powdered sugar and margarine and fold in pretzels. Press down in 9 x 13 inch pan. Bake 10 minutes at 350 degrees. Let cool.
For 2nd layer, mix cream cheese, sugar, and Cool Whip. Spread mixture on top of first layer.
For 3rd layer, dissolve Jello in boiling water with frozen strawberries. Put on 2nd layer and refrigerate.

BEEF AND VEGETABLE SOUP

2 ½ lbs beef chuck tips, cut into cubes

2 Tbsp flour

1 tsp salt

½ tsp lemon pepper

3 Tbsp butter

2 Tbsp canola oil

3 red onions, finely chopped

2 cloves minced garlic

8 carrots, sliced

2 cups sliced fresh mushrooms

2 potatoes, peeled and cubed

3 bay leaves

1 qt beef broth

2 cups burgundy or dry red wine

2 Tbsp Worcestershire sauce

Cooked noodles (opt)

Combine beef, flour, salt, and lemon pepper in a bag. Shake to coat beef. Melt butter and oil in a stock pot over medium heat. Brown beef on all sides. Remove beef and set aside, reserving pan drippings. Sauté onion and garlic in pan drippings until vegetables are tender. Add beef and remaining ingredients, stirring well. Bring to a boil. Reduce heat; cover, and simmer 1 hour. Uncover, and simmer an additional 30 minutes stirring occasionally. Discard bay leaves. Spoon into dishes or over noodles.

STEAMED BROCCOLI

1 bunch fresh broccoli

¼ cup butter, melted

1 tsp lemon pepper

1 tsp chopped chives

Juice of lemon to taste

Steam broccoli until crisp-tender, and season with butter, lemon pepper, chives, and a little lemon juice.

HERBED CRESCENT ROLLS

½ stick margarine

1 envelope Italian salad dressing mix

1 pkg refrigerated crescent rolls

Melt margarine and mix with salad dressing mix. Open rolls and separate into triangles. Brush each triangle with mixture and roll into crescent shape. Place on baking sheet and bake at 350 degrees until lightly brown. Yield: 8 rolls.

$100 FUDGE PIE

½ cup butter, melted

3 squares unsweetened chocolate

2 cups sugar

¼ tsp salt

1 tsp vanilla

4 eggs, well-beaten

⅔ cup pecans

In saucepan, melt butter and chocolate. Add sugar, salt, vanilla, and eggs. Then add pecans and put in unbaked 9-inch pie shell. Cook at 350 degrees for 30 to 40 minutes or until set.

Top: *Warming the family kettle*
Above: *Decadent Cherry and Pie - Love at first bite!*
Left: *Dinner by candlelight*

Right: A table for a king and queen
Middle: Assorted cheeses
Bottom: Enjoying the warmth of an open fire

DECADENT CHERRIES

1 (10 oz) jar maraschino cherries with stems

½ cup Southern Comfort or brandy

1 ½ cups semisweet chocolate morsels

1 Tbsp butter

Drain maraschino cherries and return to jar. Pour comfort or brandy into jar. Cover and freeze 8 hours. Drain cherries, and pat very dry. Microwave chocolate morsels and butter in a small bowl on high for 1 to 1 ½ minutes or until melted, stirring at 30 second intervals. Dip cherries quickly into melted chocolate, coating well. Place cherries on wax paper, stem sides up, and let stand until chocolate is firm. Serve immediately. Store leftovers in an airtight container in refrigerator up to 2 days.

MENU

Soups: Chicken Noodle • Skillet Orange Chili Chicken
Homemade Vegetable and Beef

Entrées: Beef with Sour Cream   Pork Chops Creole
Country Fried Steak with Gravy

Desserts: Iron Skillet Apple Pie • Skillet Peaches a la Mode
Iron Skillet Fudge Candy • Cynthia's Blueberry Tart

Cast Iron Cooking
Cabin Comfort Food

Decorations: Red and white checkered tablecloths and old quilts or bedspreads with a variety of antique china and tea cups are great ways to decorate the table. Displaying old kitchen gadgets, iron cookware, and wooden bowls in the center of the table gives the feel as if your guests are ready to cook and eat right out of the old iron skillet!

One of the greatest gifts early European settlers brought to America was the cast iron skillet. The heavy iron cookware was perfect for long-simmered meals cooked over a fire. A single cast iron skillet could cook a variety of meals with little clean up or care. It was the traditional wedding gift for a young married couple in the late 1800s and became the one essential item needed for a new bride to develop her cooking skills. With new recipes to try and old recipes passed down to her by her family, she could create mouthwatering meals for her new family. She didn't have to worry about burning the food because she knew the ironware would disperse the fire's heat evenly. She also knew that her wedding gift would only get better with time and use, and years later, she would pass it down to the next generation to continue the tradition of comfort cooking.

When uncovering the treasures of the Meador Homestead cabin, we discovered iron cookware of all sizes and shapes. Some of the skillets were hung on the wall as if to decorate the white beaded board kitchen wall but in reality, they were hung for easy reach to cook the everyday cornbread or to fry the breakfast bacon. The old iron pot, showing signs of much use, still sits today beside the fireplace. It has a dark color and thick, smooth surface. It is still used today to cook delicious chili over the Christmas Eve fire. The iron kettle sits beside it, ready to warm up water for tea, washing, or cooking armfuls of vegetables freshly picked from the family garden.

Iron cookware can withstand intense heat, so the family in earlier times could put it directly on top of a smoldering fire or later on the old pot-bellied stove. As kitchen cooking evolved, the iron cookware still was virtually indestructible and could be transferred from the stove top immediately into a hot oven. The iron absorbs flavors from one meal and releases them into the next. Consequently, the cast iron was merely wiped clean and never washed, thus seeing the surface build up in each cast ware.

My family has included a variety of food that is best cooked in cast iron cookware. We offers a chili and two soups to be cooked in a Dutch oven or large cast-iron pot to warm the body and the soul on a cold winter's night. The Chicken Soup is hearty and perfect comfort food for those who are sick or healthy. For our entrees, we have a luscious, fancy dish that is similar to a beef stroganoff, pork chops that become the center of the meal with the sides piled on top, and Country Fried Steak with gravy made from the goodness left in the pan. We have a variety of desserts from candy to an elegant way of serving fresh peaches. Our iron skillet Apple pie is a favorite of our tearoom customers. We bring the iron skillet straight from the oven and let guests serve themselves! They love it. My husband's favorite of all the desserts I make is the Blueberry tart, created by one of my mom's best friends, Cynthia Holmes. Regardless of the recipe, all you need is a strong arm and a seasoned skillet to bring joy and comfort to your family table!

CHICKEN NOODLE SOUP

3 lb chicken, skins removed

4 qt water

1 onion, quartered

2 tsp Italian seasoning

1 tsp lemon pepper

3 cloves garlic, minced

3 bay leaves

2 cups sliced carrots

2 cups celery, cut up

1 (7 oz) pkg favorite noodles

Parmesan cheese, grated (opt)

¼ cup cooking sherry (opt)

Salt and pepper to taste

2 Tbsp parsley and rosemary for garnish

Cook first 7 ingredients in a pot until chicken is tender (about 45 minutes). Remove chicken and discard bay leaves and onion. Debone chicken and cut up. Bring reserved stock back to a boil. Add carrots and celery and cook for 7 minutes. Add noodles and cook according to package directions. Add chicken and optional ingredients. Season with salt and pepper to taste. Spoon into bowl and garnish with rosemary or parsley. Yield: 8 servings.

SKILLET ORANGE CHILI CHICKEN

2 Tbsp olive oil

3 to 4 lbs boneless chicken breasts, cut into strips

1 purple onion, thinly sliced

4 garlic cloves, minced

1 ½ cups orange juice

¾ cup chicken broth

3 Tbsp chili sauce

1 ¾ cups cooked black beans with liquid

1 red bell pepper, cut into strips

1 Tbsp dark rum

Salt and pepper for seasoning

Fresh cilantro chopped for garnish

Sour cream and cheddar cheese for garnish

Heat oil in a large skillet over medium heat. Brown chicken on all sides in oil and drain on paper towels. Sauté onion in pan drippings until browned. Add garlic and sauté one minute. Return chicken to skillet and add orange juice, broth, and chili sauce. Cover and simmer over low heat 30 minutes. Add black beans with liquid and bell pepper strips. Simmer uncovered for 30 minutes. Add rum, salt, and pepper and simmer 15 minutes. Spoon into bowl, sprinkle with cilantro, add dollop of sour cream and cheese, and serve immediately. Yield: 4 to 6 servings.

Previous page: *Vintage Cast Iron Kitchen Accessories*

HOMEMADE VEGETABLE AND BEEF SOUP

2 or more quarts of water

1 Tbsp salt

1 lb bits of roast or stew meat, cut up

1 (16 oz) can stewed tomatoes with juice

1 celery stalk, chopped

1 green bell pepper, chopped

1 onion, chopped

2 medium potatoes, peeled and cubed

4 carrots, sliced

1 (6 oz) can tomato paste

1 cup okra or 6 fresh pods, chopped

1 ½ cups lima beans

1 cup corn

Seasonings:
Salt

Pepper

Hot sauce

Bay leaf

Brown sugar

Bring salted water to a boil in a large Dutch oven. Add beef, stewed tomatoes, celery, pepper, and onion. Simmer for 45 minutes. Add potatoes, carrots, tomato paste, and other vegetables of choice. Season with seasonings of choice and simmer for 1 hour.

Left: *Chicken Soup warms the soul*
Above: *Chili Chicken soothes the spirit*
Below: *Geraniums planted in an old cast iron wash pot*

155

PORK CHOPS CREOLE

4 pork loin or rib chops, ½ to ¾ inch thick

1 tsp salt

¼ tsp pepper

4 thin onion slices

4 green pepper rings

4 Tbsp uncooked instant rice

1 (8 oz) can stewed tomatoes

In 10-inch cast-iron skillet, brown chops over medium heat. Sprinkle salt and pepper on chops. Top each chop with 1 onion slice, 1 green pepper ring, 1 Tbsp rice, and ¼ cup of tomatoes. Reduce heat, cover, and simmer until done (about 45 minutes). (Add small amount of water, if necessary.)

Clockwise From Above: Southern inspired pork chops, Mouth-watering country fried steak, Meador Home stead cast iron kettle, Cast iron of Noah's Ark

BEEF WITH SOUR CREAM

1 lb lean beef round steak

¼ cup flour

Salt, pepper, and garlic powder

2 Tbsp vegetable oil

¾ cup chopped onions

1 cup beef broth

½ tsp thyme

1 (4 oz) can sliced mushrooms and liquid

1 (10 oz) pkg frozen green peas

½ cup sour cream

3 to 4 cups hot, cooked rice

Remove bone and fat from steak. Cut meat into thin, narrow strips. Dredge in flour, and seasoned with salt, pepper, and garlic powder. Heat oil in skillet. Add meat and brown. Add onions, broth, thyme, and liquid from mushrooms. Cover and simmer about 45 minutes or until meat is tender. Add mushrooms and peas. Cover and cook 5 to 7 minutes more. Stir in sour cream; heat but do not boil. Serve over hot, fluffy rice. Yield: 6 servings

COUNTRY FRIED STEAK WITH GRAVY

3 lbs boneless sirloin steak, ½ inch thick

1 Tbsp salt

1 Tbsp white vinegar

3 cups all-purpose flour

2 Tbsp ground pepper

Vegetable oil

½ cup all-purpose flour

2 cups milk

¼ tsp salt

½ tsp ground pepper

Cut steak into 10 to 12 pieces. Place in a large Ziploc bag; add water to cover. Stir in salt and vinegar. Seal and marinate in refrigerator for 2 hours. Combine 3 cups flour and pepper and stir well. Remove meat from marinade. Dredge meat in flour mixture. Pour oil to depth of 2 inches into a large heavy iron skillet and heat to 375 degrees. Fry meat, a few pieces at a time, in hot oil over medium heat 6 to 7 minutes on each side or until lightly browned. Remove from skillet and drain on paper towels. Set aside, and keep warm. Drain pan drippings, reserving 2 Tbsp drippings in skillet. Place skillet over low heat. Add ½ cup flour, stirring until smooth. Cook 1 minute, stirring constantly. Gradually add milk and cook over medium heat, stirring constantly until mixture is thickened. Stir in salt and pepper. Serve meat with gravy. Yield: 10 to 12 servings.

IRON SKILLET APPLE PIE

1 stick plus 1 Tbsp butter, divided

1 cup brown sugar

3 Pillsbury refrigerated pie crusts

5 Granny Smith apples, peeled and thinly sliced

1 ¼ cups sugar, divided

2 tsp cinnamon, divided

Melt the stick of butter in large iron skillet in 350 degree oven. Stir in brown sugar until well blended. Place 1 pie crust on top of this mixture. Place half the apple slices on top of crust. Mix ½ cup of the sugar with 1 tsp of the cinnamon, and sprinkle mixture on top of apples. Place second pie crust on top and layer remaining apple slices. Mix ½ cup of the sugar and 1 tsp of the cinnamon and sprinkle on top of apples. Place third pie crust on top. Sprinkle with ¼ cup of sugar and dot with the 1 Tbsp of butter, or more if desired. Cut small slits in top of pie crust for air. Bake at 350 degrees for 45 minutes, or until golden brown.

Clockwise from below: *The Ebenezer Stone of Meador Homestead/C.G. Meador's Cast Iron Bed, Peaches sizzling in the skillet, Served over ice cream, Making apple pie*

SKILLET PEACHES `a la MODE

1 (15 oz) refrigerated pie crust

1 Tbsp melted butter

1 Tbsp decorating or granulated sugar

¼ tsp cinnamon

⅓ cup butter, melted

6 to 8 peaches, pitted and halved or quartered

¼ cup peach nectar

2 Tbsp packed brown sugar

Blueberries, blackberries, or raspberries

Fresh mint leaves

Vanilla ice cream

Let pie crust thaw for about 15 minutes. Line baking sheet with aluminum foil or parchment paper. Unroll crust onto lightly floured surface. Brush with melted butter and sprinkle with mixture of sugar and cinnamon. Cut pastry in strips or desired shapes. Place on prepared sheet and bake for 10 to 12 minutes at 350 degrees until lightly browned. Cool on baking sheet. Pastry strips can be frozen up to 3 months. Yield: about 40 strips.

Melt butter in large skillet over medium heat. Add peaches, skin sides up. Reduce heat and cook 4 minutes, turning once. Remove peaches to bowls. Add nectar and brown sugar to skillet. Cook and stir over medium heat 1 to 2 minutes or until sugar is dissolved and syrup forms. Spoon syrup onto peaches. Top with berries, pastry strips, mint leaves, and ice cream. Yield: 6 to 8 servings.

IRON SKILLET FUDGE CANDY

2 ½ cups sugar

1 stick butter

6 oz canned milk

1 (6 oz) pkg semi-sweet chocolate pieces

1 tsp vanilla

2 cups chopped pecans

Mix sugar, butter, and milk together in a heavy iron skillet and bring to a boil. Reduce to low and cook 6 minutes, stirring occasionally. Remove from heat; add chocolate and stir until dissolved. Add vanilla, stir in pecans, and drop onto wax paper with a teaspoon. Let cool and store in an airtight container.

CYNTHIA'S BLUEBERRY TART

1 9-inch pie crust, unbaked

1 ½ cups blueberries

1 cup water

1 cup sugar

1 stick butter

Ice cream (opt)

Spray Pam on bottom and sides of a cast iron skillet. Take the pie crust and place about 1 ½ cups of blueberries in the center. Fold the pie crust over the blueberries and pinch edges. Place in cast iron skillet. In a saucepan, place 1 cup of water, 1 cup of sugar, and 1 stick of butter. Stir until dissolved over medium heat. Pour liquid over pie crust and bake for about 45 minutes at 350 degrees. Serve hot with or without ice cream.

Right: Steel casting light (c. 1900) at Meador Homestead (including the only stained glass on the property), "Jump for Joy" Cast Iron Bank

Curing Cast Iron: Cast iron items need to be cured to discourage rusting. To cure, wash all surfaces with mild soap. Dry thoroughly. Grease inside surface with solid vegetable shortening. Do not use oil, butter, or margarine. Place ironware in an oven for 350 degrees for about 1 hour. Remove piece from oven and wipe grease out with paper towels. Cool completely. Repeat process several more times. To care for your ironware, remove any food particles with a plastic scrubber after use. Wash with lukewarm water and dry the piece thoroughly in a warm oven. Coat with a thin layer of vegetable oil spray and wipe with a paper towel. Store uncovered.

Right: *Cynthia's Delight*
Below: *PawPaw and Laney enjoying iron skillet apple pie with the old cast iron water pump (c. 1913) behind*

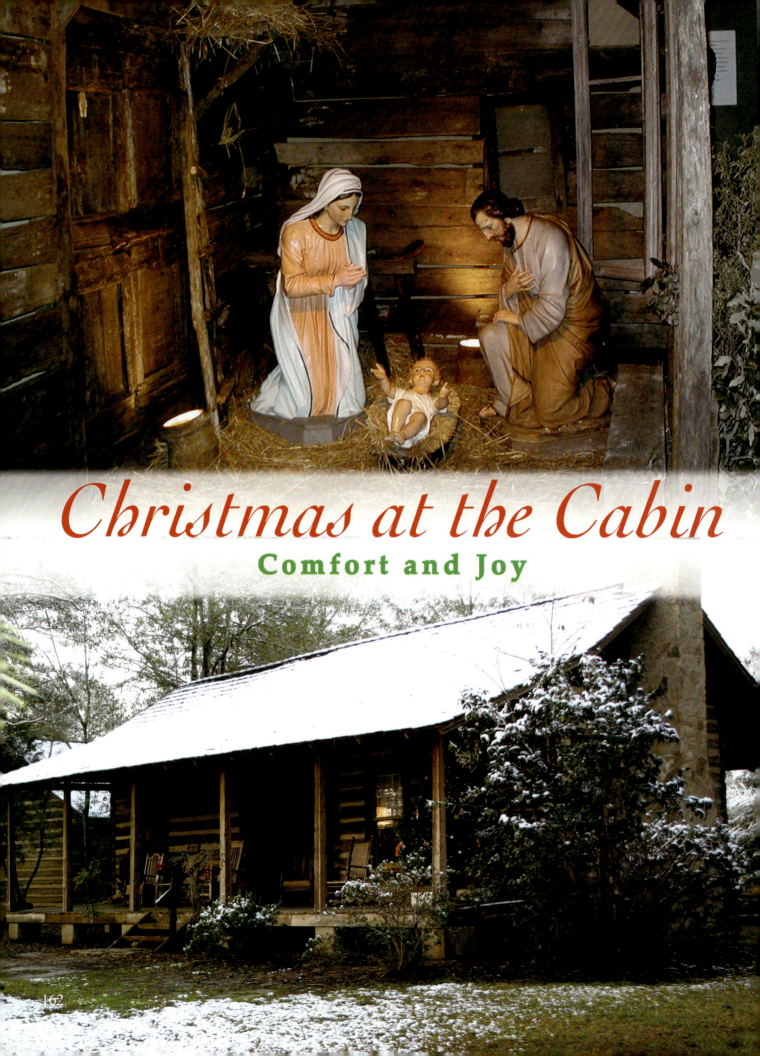

Christmas at the Cabin
Comfort and Joy

MENU

Italian Bread Soup

Salmon Green Salad with Aioli Sauce

Marinated Beef Tenderloin

Mashed Potatoes with Cheese

Broccoli Casserole

Ambrosia

Cloverleaf Refrigerator Rolls

Spud's Cocoons

White Chocolate Mousse with Strawberries

Tea: Snowflake or Gingerbread Crème

Decorations: Fruit and seasonal greenery should deck the table with Christmas ornaments or bows as napkin holders. Use Christmas boxes or bags as vases and fill them with greenery of holly or cedar and seasonal flowers.

As a young girl, I always looked forward going to my grandfather's home on Christmas Day! The cabin had always looked like an old farm house to me because, through the years, the women of the home had remodeled it several times. In 1928 when my grandfather and grandmother bought the cabin from my great-grandfather, additional rooms were added on, including an indoor kitchen and bathroom. Our Christmas spot for the family gathering was the small den in the addition where plyboard paneling had covered the wallpapers and the original logs of the 1885 cabin. There the Meador family would crowd close to the warm gas heater glowing and joyfully open gifts the relatives had brought them.

I remember my favorite present was a child's spinning wheel and yarn kit my Aunt Frances and Uncle Pete gave me. Many endless hours were tirelessly spent at my weaving frame moving the multicolored yarn in and out to make small quilts for my family. My grandfather always somehow had trouble opening his gifts, so he gave me the job of being his official "Unwrapper." We all knew what he was going to receive as I would tear into the brightly-colored packages—books and more books (he was an avid history reader) and always a box of Tampa Nugget or King Edward cigars.

After all the "Oohs" and "Aahs," the adults would proceed into the dining room, also with a gas heater, and the kids into the small white beaded-board kitchen for a bountiful buffet of food, with each family bringing their own "specialty." You could always count on my favorite dish, mashed potatoes with cheese, being served, and we all looked fondly to dessert time when we could dig into the orange, white, and cherry colors of the Christmas ambrosia shining through the beautifully cut glass container. Beside this fancy dish was another crystal plate loaded with delicious white cocoon cookies. These three delicacies were all I needed as a little girl to be completely satisfied and full of much "comfort and joy."

Today, we dress up our Christmas Cabin menu with my family's favorite food. These foods can be served for a family feast or a romantic Christmas candlelight dinner by the fire. We begin with our Italian Bread Soup. This dish is from Tuscany and the hills around beautiful Florence. It is a traditional Christmas dish that is served in Italy, and my family had the privilege of eating this frugal dish as part of a seven course meal in Greve, Italy, on New Year's Eve. The Maranated Beef Tenderloin dish is what makes our dinner an elegant affair, and the broccoli casserole can be served as an appetizer with crackers or as a side vegetable dish. Of course, we have my Christmas favorites of mashed potatoes, ambrosia, and cocoons. We call them Spud's Cocoons because one year, Spud, our springer spaniel, found these delicacies on the dessert table and ate them all. As we opened presents, he laid in a chair, literally, "sick as a dog!"

We've added an extra gift with our White Chocolate Mousse and Strawberries. We serve it in a martini glass and tie a green ribbon in a bow to bring the red, green, and white of Christmas to the table. After this meal, we are sure you will be full of the season's cheer.

Merry Christmas!

ITALIAN BREAD SOUP

4 cups chicken stock

4 cups beef stock

½ cup white wine

4 Tbsp olive oil

3 cloves garlic

1 medium yellow onion, chopped

2 ribs of celery, chopped

3 medium tomatoes, chopped

1 bay leaf

⅛ tsp red pepper flakes

¼ cup chopped basil

¼ cup chopped parsley

½ lb French bread, cubed, dry

Salt and pepper

Parmesan cheese, grated

Extra parsley, chopped

Heat the chicken stock, beef stock, and wine in a 4 to 6 quart pot. Heat a large frying pan and add 2 Tbsp of the oil and the garlic, onion, and celery. Sauté for 5 minutes. Add the tomato and sauté 5 minutes more. Add to the pot of stock along with the bay leaf, red pepper flakes, basil, and parsley. Cover and simmer 1 hour.

Heat the frying pan again and add the remaining 2 Tbsp of oil. Add the dried bread cubes and toast them until light golden brown. Do not burn. Add to the pot. Add salt and pepper to taste. Remove the bay leaf. Simmer for 15 minutes and serve with grated Parmesan cheese and chopped parsley.

SALMON GREEN SALAD WITH AIOLI SAUCE

1 pkg of smoke salmon, thinly sliced

Romaine lettuce

Boiled eggs, sliced

Tomatoes

Capers

Cut salmon slices into pieces or roll. Atop romaine lettuce leaves, place salmon and remaining ingredients as garnish. Top with aioli sauce.

Aioli Sauce:
4 garlic cloves, peeled and chopped fine

⅛ tsp sea salt

1 tsp Dijon mustard

2 egg yolks

1 cup virgin olive oil

½ tsp cold water

1 tsp lemon juice

Pinch of saffron (opt)

Use a food processor to mince garlic cloves with salt, or grind with mortar bowl and pestle. Transfer to a bowl and whisk in mustard and then the egg yolks. Add half of the oil, and slowly whisk. Once the first half of the oil is incorporated, then add the water and the lemon juice, whisking constantly. Slowly add the rest of the oil. The mixture will thicken as you continue to blend it. The mixture should be slightly thinner than commercial mayonnaise. If it becomes too thick, you can add a bit more warm water one teaspoon at a time.

*The consumption of raw or undercooked eggs may increase your risk of food-borne illness, especially to children and the elderly.

Previous page: *Christmas at Meador Homestead*
Clockwise from left: *A Winter wonderland, A culinary salad delight, "Miss Peggy" welcomes visitors*

MARINATED BEEF TENDERLOIN

1 cup ketchup

½ tsp Worcestershire sauce

2 tsp mustard

1 ½ cups water

2 envelopes Italian salad dressing mix

6-7 lbs beef tenderloin, trimmed

Watercress and grapes (opt)

Combine first 5 ingredients to make the marinade. Place meat in a Ziploc bag. Add marinade and seal. Place sealed bag in pan and refrigerate 8 hours, turning occasionally. Drain off and reserve marinade for basting. Place tenderloin on baking rack; insert meat thermometer. Bake at 425 degrees for 25 minutes and then turn to 325 degrees and continue to bake until thermometer registers 160 degrees. Baste occasionally and garnish with watercress and grapes. Yield: 8 to 10 servings.

This page: *Clockwise from above: Meador family children in live nativity scene, Simple stocking place setting, Never disappointing - Tenderloin*
Facing page: *The comfort and cheer of casseroles and potatoes Laney poses as "Baby Jesus" in church program*

BROCCOLI CASSEROLE

1 large onion, chopped

½ stick margarine

1 small can mushrooms, drained and chopped

1 (6 oz) roll of garlic cheese

2 pkgs broccoli, chopped, cooked, and drained

1 can mushroom soup

½ cup slivered almonds

Ritz cracker crumbs

Crackers of your choice (opt)

Sauté onions in ½ stick margarine. Mix in rest of ingredients, except cracker crumbs, heating until cheese is melted. Put in chafing dish and serve. If served as a casserole, top with Ritz cracker crumbs. If served as a dip (opt), put in bowl and provide crackers of your choice. Yield: 8-10 servings.

MASHED POTATOES WITH CHEESE

8 potatoes

1 stick butter

1 cup milk

Garlic salt and pepper

Cheddar cheese

Boil potatoes with peeling. After tender, peel potatoes and place in electric mixer. While still hot, put butter in mixer and let melt. Add milk and beat until creamy. Add salt and pepper to taste and top with shredded cheese.

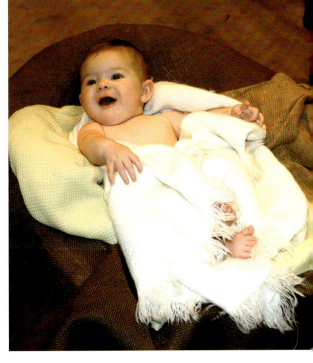

167

CLOVERLEAF REFRIGERATOR ROLLS

1 cup water

½ cup butter

4 to 5 cups all purpose-flour

½ cup sugar

2 envelopes rapid-rise yeast

1 tsp salt

3 large eggs

Combine water and butter in a saucepan. Heat until butter melts, stirring occasionally. Cool to lukewarm. Combine 2 cups flour, sugar, yeast, and salt in a large mixing bowl. Gradually add liquid mixture to flour mixture, beating at low speed with an electric mixer. Add eggs, beating until moistened. Beat 3 more minutes at medium speed. Gradually stir in enough remaining flour to make a soft dough.
Turn dough out onto a lightly floured surface and knead 3 or 4 times. Place in a large well greased bowl, turning dough to grease top. Cover and chill at least 8 hours. Punch dough down. Using one fourth of dough recipe, divide dough into 3 portions. Divide each portion into 6 pieces; shape each piece into a smooth ball. Place 3 balls in each greased muffin pan. Do same thing with the rest of dough. Cover and let rise in a warm place, free from drafts for 20 minutes or until doubled in bulk. Bake at 400 degrees for 10 to 12 minutes or until golden. Yield: 24 rolls.

AMBROSIA

12 small oranges

1 (20 oz) can crushed pineapple, undrained

2 cups grated fresh coconut

Whipped cream (opt)

Maraschino cherries, drained

Peel and section oranges, catching juice in a bowl. Add orange sections, pineapple, and coconut to juice and toss gently. Cover and chill thoroughly. Garnish with drained cherries. Spoon fruit mixture into individual dishes; top each serving with a dollop of whipped cream, if desired. Yield: 12 servings.

Clockwise from Left: *Meador dairy farm Christmas dishes, Rolls - never disappointing, Christmas cocoons, Vintage child's toy, Baby Santa, A dessert with real attitude, Grandmother's tree-topper*

SPUD'S COCOONS

1 stick margarine

2 cups flour

4 Tbsp powdered sugar

2 tsp vanilla

2 cups chopped pecans

Powdered sugar

Work butter into flour and sugar as for a pie crust with fork. Add vanilla and nuts. Take a small piece of dough about the size of an English walnut and roll between palms and shape. Bake on ungreased baking sheet in oven at 275 degrees for about 30 or 40 minutes. Slightly cool and roll in powdered sugar.

WHITE CHOCOLATE MOUSSE WITH STRAWBERRIES

8 ounces Baker's white chocolate, chopped

1 2/3 cups heavy whipping cream, divided

1/2 tsp almond extract

1 pint strawberries, hulled and sliced

1 Tbsp sugar

Heat chocolate and 2/3 cup whipping cream on low in microwave at 30 second intervals until chocolate is melted. Stir until cooled, (about 20-30 minutes). With mixer, beat remaining 1 cup whipping cream and almond extract until stiff peaks form. Fold whipped cream into chocolate mixture in 2 parts. Chill. Combine strawberries and sugar and chill. Spoon mousse into individual serving dishes and top with strawberries. Yield: 12 servings.

Anytime Celebrations

Rise and Shine
Bed and Breakfast Food

Poker Night with Price
A Game Gathering Meal

Harvest of Memories
A Come to Sunday Dinner Meal

A Friends Forever Luncheon
Feasting with Friends

A Family Gathering
Rekindling Ties with Lovin' Spoonfuls

Sewing Circle and Southern Sides
A Luncheon with Special Friends

Menu
Pear Preserves
Creole Breakfast Bread Pudding
Creamy Grits
Country Ham with Redeye Gravy
Pecan Waffles
Cinnamon Pecan Rolls
Quick Buttermilk Biscuits
English Muffin French Toast
Sour Cream Coffee Cake
Simple French Toast
Effie's Apple Muffins
Buttery Cinnamon Skillet Apples

Rise and Shine
(Bed and Breakfast Food)

Decorations: Make this a casual breakfast table to greet guests to another day. Flowers, the morning paper, and good food are all you need, with coffee and tea ready to pour!

The oldest piece of furniture in the Meador Homestead cabin is the old double-rope bed. It was made by my great-great-great-grandfather as a wedding present for his bride in 1856. It would probably have been forgotten except my grandfather remembered this beautiful gift of love. After much searching, he found the bed in the old 1885 barn where cows were using it as a trough from which to eat their morning meal. He cleaned up the handmade carved bed and brought it to the cabin, and for at least half a century and more, it has remained in the same corner of the south room, inviting guests to spend the night. It was the place I slept as a child when I would visit my grandparents for the night, and today, this is the spot where our Bed and Breakfast guests lay their heads. It's a lot more comfortable now since we've replaced the ropes and the straw-stuffed seed bag with a mattress. Now when we say, "Sleep tight and don't let the bed bugs bite," it's just a pleasant formality of hoping our visitors will sleep comfortably. They do, and when light breaks forth into morning, they arrive at the breakfast table having had a good night's sleep.

My father would fondly tell us about his youth and morning times at the cabin. During the winter months and beyond, he would arise each morning to a frosty wave of cold air rushing through the cracks in the heart pine floor. With the smell of hot biscuits cooking, he would bounce out of bed and "bare feet run" to the old wood-burning stove in the kitchen. There he would find Lillie Belle, the family cook, waiting for him to warm him with a hot meal before his daily chore of milking the cows began. Throughout his life, he never talked about the day's beginning as being dreaded or drearisome, but rather glorified it as a cherished memory of his young life on the farm. Listening to him, I was always warmed by his affection towards the setting, the people, and the lessons he learned as a young man.

Today at Meador Homestead, we try to create those same cozy and pleasant feelings my father had. At the first "rise and shine," guests may choose from a variety of morning meals to warm them up for their day's activities. If you're interested in a breakfast casserole filled with eggs, cheese, and sausage, we have included our Creole Breakfast Bread Pudding. As a child, I loved French toast and would make it from a recipe out of a Betty Crocker cookbook for

children. In our menu, I have included two recipes for this French breakfast delight. One is a simple toast, but I make it "adult" by adding some Grand Marnier. The English Muffin Toast is a healthy spin using buttermilk, yogurt, and powerful antioxidant fruit. Our Pecan waffles are out of this world, along with the Skillet Cinnamon Rolls and my Great-Aunt Ruby's Coffee Cake. We also have included a recipe for apple muffins to serve with any meal, along with a hot apple fruit dish as a breakfast dessert.

Grits have been served at the Southern breakfast table for centuries, along with the other Southern staple: biscuits. We have included our easy biscuit recipe and also our pear preserve recipe. My great-grandmother used the pears from the century-old pear tree in the front yard, and now I am following in Ms. Lena's footsteps by making the delicious preserves. Satisfied from a scrumptious breakfast and peaceful sleep, our overnight friends are free to take home some of the pears as a special token of their time at the cabin. That is, if the rabbits and deer haven't eaten the juicy fruit already for their breakfast. It suffices to say that all God's creatures enjoy breakfast at the cabin. We hope you do too!

PEAR PRESERVES

16 cups sliced pears, peeled

4 cups sugar

Juice of lemon, about ½ cup

2 cups of water

Place pears, sugar, and lemon juice in a large pot and add 2 cups of water. Cook over moderate heat until pears are tender and syrup is thick (about 30 to 45 minutes) or until desired consistency. Use potato masher to mash the pears as they cook. Put in jars and chill.

CREOLE BREAKFAST BREAD PUDDING

½ lb breakfast pan sausage

½ cup minced yellow onions

¼ cup minced green bell pepper

⅓ cup sliced green onions

⅓ cup dry white wine

8 cups day-old French bread (torn into 1 inch cubes)

2 ½ cups milk

½ cup heavy cream

¼ cup melted butter

8 large eggs, beaten

½ lb pepper jack cheese, grated

½ lb Monterey jack cheese, grated

¾ tsp salt

⅛ tsp freshly ground black pepper

½ tsp cayenne

¾ cup sour cream

½ cup grated Parmesan cheese

Preheat oven to 325 degrees. Put sausage in hot pan and cook until golden brown and the fat is rendered, about 5 minutes. Add the onions and bell peppers, and sauté until soft (about 3 minutes). Add the green onions and stir well. Add the white wine and reduce slightly, stirring, about 1 minute over high heat. Remove from heat. Place the bread in a large mixing bowl. Add the milk and cream and stir well. Let sit for 5 minutes. Pour the melted butter into a 10 x 13 inch casserole dish, and coat the sides and bottom evenly. Pour any extra butter into the bread mixture. Add the sausage mixture to the bread mixture. Add the eggs, grated cheeses, salt, black pepper, cayenne pepper, and quickly fold mixture together. Pour into casserole dish, cover with aluminum foil, and bake for 1 hour. Uncover and bake for 15 minutes. Remove the casserole from the oven and increase the temperature to 375 degrees. Spread the sour cream evenly over the top and cover with grated Parmesan. Bake uncovered for 10 to 15 minutes, or until the casserole is lightly browned on top. Serve hot.

Previous page: *Cinnamon Rolls worth waking up for, Southern "flavors' to indulge in..., 1856 Rope Bed*
Clockwise from left: *Pa excited for his morning chores, The cabin's original sugar cane grinding stone, Pears from the century-old pear tree, Butterfly's breakfast*

CREAMY GRITS

2 cups milk

2 cups water

1 tsp salt and pepper

1 cup uncooked regular grits

1 cup whipping cream

¼ cup butter

Bring milk, water, salt, and pepper to boil in a saucepan. Stir in grits. Reduce heat and simmer for 30 to 40 minutes, stirring occasionally until thickened. Add cream and butter and stir, simmering for 5 minutes. Yield: 6 servings.

COUNTRY HAM WITH REDEYE GRAVY

½ lb ham

1 cup black tea or coffee

⅛ cup brown sugar

Cook ham in a cast iron skillet over medium heat for 5 minutes until both sides are browned. Remove ham and reserve drippings. To make the gravy, add mixture of tea and sugar to ham drippings in skillet, stirring for about 10 minutes. Serve the gravy with the ham. Can also serve the gravy over grits (from previous recipe).

Food: Bed & Breakfast guests love our Farmer's Breakfast
Below Right: Dairy can from Homestead's original Dairy Farm
Far Right: Serious business - Breakfast Makin'!

PECAN WAFFLES

2 ½ cups all-purpose flour

1 ½ Tbsp sugar

1 Tbsp plus 1 tsp baking powder

¾ tsp salt

2 large eggs, beaten

2 ¼ cups milk

¾ cup vegetable oil

½ cup ground pecans

Combine first 4 ingredients in a large bowl. Beat eggs until smooth. In a separate bowl, combine eggs, milk, and oil; add to flour mixture. Stir in pecans. Put mixture in a preheated, oiled waffle iron, serving by serving.

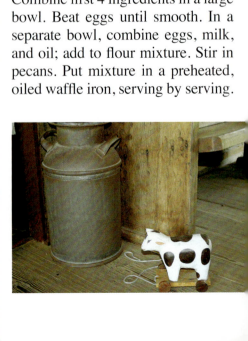

CINNAMON PECAN ROLLS

1 cup chopped pecans

1 (16 oz) pkg Pillsbury Hot Roll Mix

½ cup butter, softened

1 cup firmly packed light brown sugar

2 tsp ground cinnamon

1 cup powdered sugar

2 Tbsp milk

1 tsp vanilla extract

Preheat oven to 350 degrees. Bake pecans in a shallow pan for 5 to 7 minutes until toasted, stirring halfway through. Prepare hot roll dough as directed on package; let dough stand 5 minutes. Roll dough in a 15 x 10 inch rectangle and spread with softened butter. Stir together brown sugar and cinnamon and sprinkle over butter. Sprinkle pecans over brown sugar mixture. Roll up tightly, starting at one long end; cut into 12 slices. Place rolls, cut sides down, in a lightly greased 12 inch cast-iron skillet or 13 x 9 inch pan. Cover loosely with plastic wrap and a cloth towel; let rise in a warm place for 30 minutes or until doubled in bulk. Preheat oven to 375 degrees. Uncover rolls, and bake for 20 to 25 minutes or until center rolls are golden brown and done. Let cool in pan on a wire rack. Stir together powdered sugar, milk, and vanilla for a creamy glaze and drizzle over rolls.

QUICK BUTTERMILK BISCUITS

½ cup butter or margarine, softened

2 cups self-rising flour

¾ cup buttermilk

Flour for rolling dough

Butter, melted

Cut butter into flour. Add buttermilk. Form dough into a ball and roll on floured surface to ¾ inch thickness. Cut into desired shape and bake on lightly greased sheet for 13 to 15 minutes at 425 degrees. Brush with melted butter. Yield: 1 dozen biscuits.

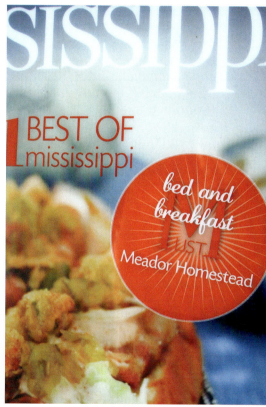

Food: French toast, Apples, and a delicious spread...Ready to get up yet?!
Bottom Right: Easter Lillies & hydrangeas welcome one to a morning rock

ENGLISH MUFFIN FRENCH TOAST

4 large eggs

1 cup nonfat buttermilk

2 tsp orange zest

1 tsp vanilla extract

6 English muffins, split

1 cup fat-free Greek yogurt

2 Tbsp maple syrup

Strawberries and nectarines, chopped

Whisk together first 4 ingredients in a bowl. Place English muffins in a baking dish, overlapping the edges of the muffins. Pour egg mixture over muffins. Cover and chill overnight. Remove muffins from remaining liquid. Cook muffins in a large skillet coated with cooking spray over medium heat 2 to 3 minutes on each side until golden brown. Stir together yogurt and syrup until blended; Top muffin with fruit and yogurt syrup and extra muffin top.

SOUR CREAM COFFEE CAKE

Batter:
1 stick butter

1 cup sugar

2 whole eggs

1 cup commercial sour cream

2 cups flour

1 tsp baking soda

1 tsp baking powder

1 tsp vanilla

Topping:
½ cup sugar

1 cup nuts

2 tsp cinnamon

In a mixing bowl, combine first 8 ingredients to make cake batter. Put ½ of mixture in greased tube pan. Sprinkle ½ topping on batter. Add rest of batter and cover with remaining topping. Bake at 350 degrees for 35 minutes.

SIMPLE FRENCH TOAST

4-6 slices French bread, cut ¾ inch thick

2 eggs

½ cup milk

1 Tbsp Grand Marnier

¼ tsp cinnamon

½ Tbsp granulated sugar (1 ½ tsp)

⅛ tsp salt

¼ tsp vanilla extract

2 Tbsp butter or margarine

Syrup

Powdered sugar

Arrange bread slices in a single layer in a shallow 2 quart baking dish. Beat eggs, milk, Grand Marnier, cinnamon, granulated sugar, salt, and vanilla together. Pour over bread in baking dish. Turn slices so that each slice is thoroughly coated. Cover and refrigerate overnight. Heat 2 Tbsp of the butter in a skillet over moderately high heat (about 350 degrees). Cook slices of bread until golden brown. Turn and cook on a second side, until browned. Add more butter if needed. Sprinkle with powdered sugar. If French bread is large in diameter, use 4 slices; if small, use 6 slices. Allow 2 to 3 slices per serving.

EFFIE'S APPLE MUFFINS

1 cup sugar

¼ cup oil

2 eggs

1 ½ cup flour

1 tsp cinnamon

1 tsp salt

BUTTERY CINNAMON SKILLET APPLES

⅓ cup sweet cream butter

1 ½ cup water

½ to ¾ cup sugar

¼ to ½ tsp cinnamon

2 tbsp cornstarch

4 medium apples, cored, unpeeled, cut in half

1 tsp vanilla

2 cups chopped apples

1 cup chopped walnuts

In a large mixing bowl, combine all ingredients. Fill muffin tins but not too full. Bake at 350 degrees for 20 to 25 minutes.

In a 10 inch skillet, melt butter over medium heat. Stir in sugar and cornstarch; mix well. Add remaining ingredients. Cover and cook over medium heat, spooning sauce over apples occasionally, until apples are fork tender and sauce is thickened (12 to 15 minutes). To serve, place 2 apple halves in individual dish and spoon ½ cup sauce over each of the halves.

POKER NIGHT WITH PRICE

A Game Gathering Meal

MENU

John Buckley's Shrimp Dip

Caesar Iceberg Wedges

Rusty's Gumbo

Parmesan Cheese Breadsticks

Chocolate Pie

Mint Julep Sweet Tea

Decorations: It is ideal to have a poker table, but any game table with cards, poker chips, etc. for a centerpiece will do. The idea is to make a fun setting for the poker, bridge, or backgammon group or even after a day's play at tennis, croquet, or golf.

My dad loved to play cards, so much that every Wednesday afternoon, you could find him at his favorite spot, the Hattiesburg Country Club, wheeling and dealing with his pals in the old poker game. He was a master at playing and always quick to share his secrets of "when to hold and when to fold" with his family and friends. He loved to win, but he was forever fair in his dealings, whether it was cards or business. One of my fond memories as a young girl with my father was learning how to play gin rummy. I always felt so special that he would take time out after a busy day's work to play with me. Unlike most parents, he only let me win once in a while and taught me that losing was just as much a part of the game. I didn't realize then, but now I know he was also teaching me how to play the game called life.

Papa Price was an avid sports fan, on the field and off. He played every sport that was available to him, from basketball to baseball. When WWII broke out, he joined quickly, ready to do his part. Although he was never shipped overseas, he did his fair share of fighting by playing baseball at seven different colleges for the navy team. He was an avid golfer, and at the age of 50, he took up the game of tennis, enjoying every moment that his young adversaries would frantically try to return his famous curve shot. My fondest memory playing tennis with him was when we won the Century Tournament (ages of partners had to add up to 100 or more). I still have the Metamucil Trophy we won for the prize.

Papa Price loved to have fun. He had the Meador wit and always a twinkle in his eye. And attitude? Whether it was a losing day at the boats, horse races, or football games, he still managed to say, "Tomorrow, my ship will come in." If a business deal went bad, he would dust himself off and plunge forward with another plan. His positive outlook on life is a trait I hope I am passing on to generations after me. We saw a little bit of his fun spirit when we were restoring the cabin in 2009. As we tore away the sheetrock and wallpaper in my dad's bedroom, we found between the 1884 logs where the chinking had fallen out—you guessed it—a deck of cards. That deck now sits on the family bookshelf, another piece of the spirit of the Meador family. The old poker table where my father and his friends played into the wee hours of the night at my home on the hill was found in the cabin behind the 1856 bed. We decided to keep it just the way it was—very war torn. It sits now with a wooden cover in the area where my dad's bedroom had been. He's probably up in heaven smiling right now, ready for another game!

Our menu is created with some of my dad's soul-satisfying favorites and can be served for any game group, whether it be after a game of golf, tennis, poker, bridge, or bunko. Dad loved seafood, and we start off with John Buckley's famous Shrimp dip. He was always faithful to order the simple Iceberg Lettuce wedge with dressing at the casinos. We commemorate those times of going with him to the boat with this dish. Rusty's Gumbo is all you need for a one-item meal. Crackers are fine on the side of the gumbo, or even French bread, but our Parmesan Cheese Sticks offer a tasty alternative and are easy to prepare. Finally, we finish with Papa Price's favorite dessert, Chocolate pie. Even if your guests have the losing hand, they'll still come back for more of these glorious game foods!

JOHN BUCKLEY'S SHRIMP DIP

1 (8 oz) pkg cream cheese

2 Tbsp sour cream

6 oz mayonnaise

Lemon juice (half of lemon)

Splashes of Worcestershire

1 Tbsp horseradish

Mustard to taste

1 cup baby shrimp, cut

Crackers of choice

Mix all well. Put in shrimp that has been cut up. Serve with crackers. Yield: 8 servings.

RUSTY'S GUMBO

Shrimp stock:

5 lbs uncooked shrimp with shells (the smaller, the better)

Tony Chachere's Original Creole Seasoning

½ medium onion, cut in 3 pieces

1 celery stalk, cut into 3 pieces

Peel and save shrimp shells. Sprinkle and season shrimp with Tony Chachere's Original Creole Seasoning. Put shells in pot with water. Add onion and celery. Simmer 30 minutes until it boils. Pour through strainer and save stock (can freeze). While this is cooking, cut up rest of ingredients for roux.

Roux:

1 cup vegetable oil

1 cup flour

2 cups chopped frozen okra

2 medium onions, chopped (about 2 cups)

1 bell pepper, chopped

3-4 celery stalks, chopped

3 tomatoes, chopped

3 bay leaves

3-4 cloves garlic, chopped

1 tsp salt

3 pinches cayenne pepper

Shrimp stock (from above)

2 Tbsp Worcestershire Sauce

Bunch of green onion, chopped

2 containers crabmeat

Cooked rice

Heat oil at medium heat. Add flour gradually and stir until medium dark or a brown color. Add okra, onions, bell pepper, and celery. Put on low and simmer for 10 minutes. Add tomatoes, bay leaves, and garlic. Add salt, cayenne, shrimp stock, and Worcestershire. Simmer 15 minutes more. Add shrimp and cook until pink. Add bunch of chopped green onion. Cook 13 minutes on medium high. Add crabmeat and cook 5 minutes more. Serve over rice.

Previous page: *Price and his favorite games*
Left: *Papa Price with his playful grin and scrumptious Shrimp Dip*
Above: *Lip-smackin' gumbo & breadsticks*

CAESAR ICEBERG WEDGES

1 or 2 small head iceberg lettuce, cut into wedges

Caesar dressing

4 to 6 bacon slices, cooked and crumbled

Freshly ground pepper to taste

Parmesan cheese, shredded

Pour dressing evenly over each lettuce wedge. Cook bacon well. Crumble when cool enough to handle. Sprinkle evenly with bacon, pepper, and cheese.

PARMESAN CHEESE BREADSTICKS

½ cup freshly grated Parmesan cheese

¼ tsp paprika

⅛ tsp ground cumin

1 (11 oz) can refrigerated breadsticks

3 Tbsp butter

Combine cheese, paprika, and cumin. Unroll breadstick dough and separate into 12 strips. Gently pull each strip to a length of 12 inches. Brush both sides of each strip with the butter and dredge in cheese mixture. Twist each strip, and place on a lightly greased baking sheet. Bake at 400 degrees for 8 to 10 minutes or until golden brown. Yield: 12 breadsticks.

Above: Chess or a game of cards (even in Italy) evoke a healthy appetite
Left: Iceberg Wedge
Right: Sweet Tea & my Dad's Favorite pie

CHOCOLATE PIE

1 9-inch pie shell

¾ cup sugar

3 Tbsp flour

3 Tbsp cocoa

1 ½ cups milk

3 egg yolks, beaten

Pinch of salt

1 tsp vanilla

1 Tbsp butter

3 egg whites

2 Tbsp sugar

Cook pie shell according to directions on package. Mix dry ingredients together well. Scald the milk by heating until a skim forms on it. Gradually add the hot milk to the dry ingredients and stir until dissolved. Place in double boiler over water and cook, stirring constantly until the mixture begins to thicken. Add the beaten egg yolks. Do this by adding some of the hot mixture to the eggs first, stirring constantly; then adding it back to the hot mixture slowly, stirring constantly so that eggs will not cook in small particles. Cook until thick. Remove from stove and add salt, vanilla, and butter. Cool and then pour into pie crust. Use a glass or metal mixing bowl. Mix room temperature egg whites and add sugar slowly. Increase speed of mixer once sugar is incorporated, and whip on high to a soft peak. Top with meringue and brown in a 350 degree oven. It is best to turn off oven and leave pie in oven until meringue is dry. Removing too soon, especially on a humid day, will cause the meringue to become chewy.

MINT JULEP SWEET TEA

½ cup fresh mint leaves

1 lemon, sliced

2 Tbsp sugar

3 cups cold sweetened tea

1 cup bourbon

Fresh mint leaves as garnish

Combine first 3 ingredients in a pitcher. Press mint leaves against sides of pitcher with back of spoon to release flavors. Stir in tea and bourbon. Serve over crushed ice and garnish.

I was born to be a teacher. I was so determined in that thought that every day after school, I would get off the bus and diligently walk to the little "schoolhouse" behind the cabin to teach. The Meador family at that time deemed that raising quail would be of financial good to the family. I, oblivious to all this as a young girl, only believed that they had graciously built the house to be my schoolroom and provided the quail to be my captive audience in practicing my teaching skills. I had a lot of disciplinary problems with my students, as they would never stop talking while I was reading or having spelling lessons, but I didn't mind. I had grown to love the little chatterers, just like my teachers at school cared for me.

My teaching days, however, suddenly came to a stop when the family came to a special Sunday meal at the cabin. As I was savoring the wild and smoky taste of the meat, I overheard terrible news. The food I was indeed enjoying was one of my students. To this day I can remember where I was sitting at the table and the sickness I felt in my stomach when this revelation occurred.

Methodist minister Pierce Harris once said, "Memory is a child walking along a seashore. You never can tell what small pebble it will pick up and store away among its treasured things." The foods in this menu are the pebbles I have picked up along the way. Each food brings to mind the person who created the recipe, the event

Harvest of Memories

A Come to Sunday Dinner Meal

MENU

Cranberry Salad • Navy Bean Soup

Smothered Quail • Tuna Fish Casserole

Red Rice • Whole Grain Pan Rolls

Green Bean Casserole

Southern Peas • Toll House Cupcakes

Ms. Lena's Sugar Cookies

Checkerboard Cake

Chocolate Butter Icing

Southern Sweet Tea

Weidmann's Blackbottom Pie

Decorations: We use family pottery vases and milk bottles from the dairy for flowers. Make this a buffet-style meal, so the family can see and share the harvest of memory food!

or place where the food was shared, and always a warm feeling in the heart as well as in the stomach—thus a Harvest of Memories.

The Navy Bean Soup was a favorite recipe of my step-grandmother, Jessie. Cranberry Salad, a recipe from my mother, has been served at every Thanksgiving and Christmas dinner for as long as I can remember. My grandfather's favorite food of all time was a cup of rice with Southern field peas from the garden. He would sit at the head of the family table and calmly sip his pea broth, as satisfyingly as if he were drinking the finest of all wines.

The Tuna Fish Casserole reminds me of my sister Nancy who made this easy and delicious dish for a family meal, only to realize she had neglected to include the main ingredient, the tuna fish! To this day, we still laugh and talk about this wonderful cooking disaster moment. Another memory with my sister was making Toll House cookies and carefully placing only 3 chocolate chips on top of each cookie to save money. We still look forward to making these cookies today, but now we pour the whole bag of chips in. I have done a variation of this recipe, with our Toll House Cookie Cupcakes, which is still sure to please.

Remember the smell and taste of those marvelous lunchroom rolls served in every school? My other grandmother, Nannie Elizabeth Caperton Steadman, was Director of Cafeterias for the Hattiesburg Schools for over 25 years. The recipe for our rolls makes me think fondly of her. They are tasty and healthy and still conjure up the wonderful smell of rising bread in the cafeteria!

Pauline Smith, Eddie's mom, faithfully made him a Checkerboard Cake for all his birthdays, and we have to include the favorite food from the Meador Homestead cabin, Ms. Lena's Sugar Cookies. Finally, we include Blackbottom Pie from the famous Weidmann's Restaurant in Meridian, MS. As a family, we always ate here when visiting or passing through Meridian. Oh, what a harvest of memories! Enjoy!

SMOTHERED QUAIL

8 quail, dressed

½ cup butter or margarine

¼ cup all-purpose flour

2 cups chicken broth

½ cup dry sherry

1 tsp salt

¾ tsp pepper

Brown quail in batches in butter in a large skillet over medium heat. Place quail, breast side up, in a lightly greased baking dish. Add flour to skillet, stirring until smooth. Cook for 2 minutes, stirring constantly over medium heat. Gradually stir in broth and sherry; cook over medium heat, stirring constantly, until mixture is thickened and bubbly. Stir in salt and pepper. Pour sauce over quail. Bake quail, covered, at 350 degrees for 1 hour. Yield: 8 servings.

NAVY BEAN SOUP

1 pound navy beans

2 qts boiling water

2 ham hocks or a ham bone

¼ cup chopped onion

½ cup chopped celery

Garlic salt

Pepper

Wash beans; place in a large bowl and add boiling water. Let beans soak for a few hours. Simmer ham bone with the beans in a large pot until beans are tender. Remove bone and take ham from the bone. Add chopped onions and celery. Add water to make about 1 gallon. Add ham meat, and seasonings to taste. Cook about 30 minutes longer. Yield: 12 servings

Previous page: *Grandmother Annie Dean teaching memories at Meador Homestead* **Clockwise from below:** *Quail divine plate, Quail (my awesome student?), A buffet of memories, Tuna casserole, Red rice-memories never tasted so good!*

TUNA FISH CASSEROLE

1 can of tuna fish

1 can of cream of mushroom soup

1 can of chow mein noodles

Shredded cheddar cheese for top

In a small casserole dish, mix tuna fish, soup, and noodles. Put cheese on top and bake at 350 degrees until the cheese melts (20-25 minutes).

RED RICE

½ lb bacon

2 cups long grain white rice

2 cups ripe, peeled, and chopped tomatoes

1 tsp salt

1 qt chicken stock

Fry bacon in a saucepan until crisp. Crumble and reserve. Pour off all but ¼ cup of grease. Add rice and sauté. Peel and chop tomatoes. Add salt, tomatoes, and chicken stock and bring to a boil. Cover and cook for 20 to 30 minutes on low until rice is tender. Add bacon.

WHOLE GRAIN PAN ROLLS

1 cup water

¼ cup honey

¼ cup butter or margarine

¾ cup whole wheat flour

½ cup regular oats, uncooked

2 pkgs dry yeast

1 tsp salt

1 egg

2 ¼ to 2 ½ cups all-purpose flour for kneading

Combine water, honey, and butter in a small saucepan; heat until butter melts. Cool. Combine wheat flour, oats, yeast, and salt in a large mixing bowl; stir well. Gradually add liquid mixture, beating at low speed of an electric mixer 1 minute. Add egg, and beat an additional 2 minutes at medium speed. Gradually add all-purpose flour to make a soft dough. Turn dough out onto a heavily floured surface and knead until smooth and elastic (about 8 minutes). Shape dough into 24 balls; place in a lightly greased 13 x 9 x 2 inch pan. Cover and let rise in a warm place, free from drafts, for 1 hour or until doubled in bulk. Bake at 375 degrees for 20 minutes or until rolls are lightly-browned. Yield: 2 dozen.

SOUTHERN PEAS

1 quart field, Crowder, or lady peas

½ to 1 cup lean ham, chunked with rind removed

1 Tbsp vegetable oil or bacon grease

2 to 3 cups ham stock, chicken broth, or water

⅓ cup chopped onion (opt)

Salt and black pepper to taste

To prepare peas, put them in a large bowl of cold water and take out any trash or hard peas that rise to the top. Wash peas and drain. In a saucepan, brown ham in vegetable oil for about 5 minutes. Add peas to ham and cover with stock, broth, or water. Add onion if desired. Cover and simmer until tender. Season with salt and pepper. As the peas cook, always add broth to keep peas covered. In general, most fresh peas will cook in 30 to 40 minutes and sometimes quicker. Peas that have been blanched and frozen will cook faster than fresh.

GREEN BEAN CASSEROLE

2 cans of green bean

¾ cup milk

1 (10 ¾ oz) can cream of mushroom soup

1 ½ cups French fried onions, divided

Salt

Pepper

Clockwise from above: Green Bean Casserole, "Pa" under pear tree w/ hat, cigar in hand, & best friend "Squeaky", A Homestead classic sugar cookies, Pa's Pea Soup, Meador family celebrating W.P. Meador's 90th birthday (Who's the one with the finger in her mouth?)

In a greased 1 ½ qt casserole, combine all ingredients except ¾ cup of French fried onions. Bake at 350 degrees for about 30 minutes. Top with remaining onions and bake for 5 minutes or until onions are golden.
Yield: 6 servings.

TOLL HOUSE CUPCAKES

1st layer:

½ cup butter

6 Tbsp sugar

6 Tbsp dark brown sugar

½ tsp vanilla

1 egg

1 cup plus 2 Tbsp flour

½ tsp baking soda

½ tsp salt

2nd layer:

½ cup dark brown sugar

1 egg

⅛ tsp salt

6 oz chocolate chips

½ cup pecans or walnuts, chopped

½ tsp vanilla

Cream together the butter, sugars, and vanilla. Beat in egg. Add flour, baking soda, and salt. Put soupspoon amount of mixture in paper-lined standard muffin pan. Cook 10 to 12 minutes at 350 degrees. Remove from oven while still soft and hit in middle with spoon. Mix ½ cup brown sugar, egg, and salt. Then stir in chocolate chips, nuts, and tsp vanilla. Add 1 Tbsp of mixture to each cupcake. Bake 15 more minutes.

MS. LENA'S SUGAR COOKIES

½ cup butter

1 cup sugar

2 tsp vanilla

1 egg

1 ¼ cup flour

½ tsp baking soda

½ tsp salt

½ cups finely chopped nuts

Sugar for topping

Cream butter and sugar. Add vanilla and other ingredients. Put spoonfuls of mixture onto a baking sheet and bake at 350 degrees until slightly brown. Press sugar on top of cooked cookies immediately after coming out of the oven.

CRANBERRY SALAD

1 (3 ¾ oz) pkg orange jello

1 cup sliced cranberries

¾ cup sugar

1 can crushed pineapple, drained

1 cup diced apples

1 cup chopped nuts

Mix jello according to directions on package. In a separate serving dish, mix cranberries with ¾ cup sugar and pineapple. Let stand a few minutes. Then add jello, diced apples, and chopped nuts. Refrigerate until serving.

CHECKERBOARD CAKE

3 oz semisweet chocolate

4 cups sifted cake flour

2 cups sugar

2 tsp baking powder

1 ½ tsp salt

1 cup unsalted butter, softened

1 ⅓ cups milk, divided

1 Tbsp vanilla

4 eggs

Melt chocolate. In a large mixing bowl, combine flour, sugar, baking powder, and salt. Mix on low speed for 1 minute, until well blended. Add butter and 1 cup of milk and beat at medium speed for 1 ½ minutes, scraping down sides of bowl. In another bowl, combine vanilla, eggs, and remaining ⅓ cup of milk and beat lightly. Add to batter in 3 parts, beating at medium speed for 20 seconds after each addition. Scrape down sides of bowl after each part. Divide batter in half. Stir melted chocolate into one half of batter until uniform in color.

Preheat oven to 350 degrees. Grease and flour bottoms and sides of 3 9-inch cake pans. Place checkerboard divider into one prepared pan. Then pour in the two batters (light and dark), alternating colors. Pour light batter in the outside ring, dark in the middle ring, and light in the center. Repeat for second pan but reverse the order of colors. Remove dividers. Place pans in the center of the oven and bake 25 minutes. Cool cakes on racks 10 minutes. Use a very thin layer of icing between layers so you won't upset the checkerboard effect.

CHOCOLATE BUTTER ICING

3 oz baking chocolate

6 Tbsp milk

3 cups powdered sugar

6 Tbsp butter

Dash of salt

1 Tbsp vanilla

Melt chocolate. In a saucepan, heat milk to boiling, remove from heat, add powdered sugar all at once, and beat until smooth. Add melted chocolate and cool to lukewarm. In a mixing bowl, beat butter until creamy. Add salt, vanilla, and cooled chocolate mixture and beat vigorously. Spread at once. Yield is sufficient for a 3-layer cake.

WEIDMANN'S BLACKBOTTOM PIE
(WEIDMANN' RESTAURANT, MERIDIAN, MS, SINCE 1870)

2 cups crushed ginger snaps

5 Tbsp melted butter

2 cups milk, scalded

4 egg yolks, beaten

½ cup sugar

1 ½ Tbsp cornstarch

1 ½ squares bitter chocolate

1 tsp vanilla

1 Tbsp gelatin

2 tsp cold water

4 egg whites

½ cup sugar

¼ tsp cream of tartar

2 Tbsp whiskey

Whipped cream and chocolate shavings

Add melted butter to crushed ginger snaps. Pat into 9-inch pie pan. Bake in 400 degree oven 10 minutes and cool. Add egg slowly to hot milk. Combine sugar and cornstarch and stir into egg mixture. Cook in double boiler for 20 minutes, stirring occasionally, until it coats spoon. Remove, and take out one cup. Add chocolate to cup you removed; beat well as it cools. Add vanilla, and then pour this mixture into pie crust. Chill. Dissolve gelatin, cold water, and add remaining custard and cool. Beat egg whites with sugar until stiff. Add cream of tartar and whiskey. Fold into plain custard mixture and pour on top of chocolate mixture. Chill. Cover top of pie with whipped cream and shavings of chocolate. Keep chilled.

Facing page: *Eddie's favorite birthday cake*
Top: *Papa Price's initials in the old water well*
Middle: *"PawPaw" & "Cupcake" Emily Trick-or-Treating*
Bottom: *Even an old shovel can be made into a memory - A Fairy Garden*

SOUTHERN SWEET TEA

3 cups water

2 family-size tea bags

¾ cup sugar

7 cups cold water

Bring 3 cups water to a boil; add tea bags. Boil for 1 minute, remove, and cover. Steep for 10 minutes. Discard tea bags. Add sugar, stirring until dissolved. Pour into a 1 gallon container or pitcher. Add 7 cups of cold water. Serve over ice.

A Friends Forever Luncheon

Feasting with Friends

MENU
Cold Spiced Tea
Shrimp Julep
Deviled Eggs
Steamed Vegetables
Grilled Chicken Over Almond and Orange Green Salad
Banana Bread
Easy Boiled Custard
Friendship Cake
Brandied Fruit Starter

Decorations: Use cards of friendship as name cards. Make it a festive feel with colorful zinnias and bright-colored plates. Quotes of friendship can be displayed on the table. Place zinnias on colorful napkins in place of napkin rings. For those special friends, you will want to break out the silver. For our traditional shrimp cocktail, we used silver julep cups to give the occasion an extra beautiful feel.

In the recipe for friendship bread [cake] in our menu, my mother-in-law writes to her sister in 1980: "This 'Starter' you have, Jerry, can last through generations. I started yours from start." How appropriate to eat a bread with part of it [Brandied Fruit Starter] to last for many years to come! Isn't that the way it is with true friendship? A true friend's love will last forever. Unlike a marriage where vows are taken and commitments are made, there is no need to sign an oath of loyalty for friendship. "A good friend is a connection to life—a tie to the past, a road to the future, the key to sanity in a totally insane world." -Wyse

I have been blessed to have a host of true friends in my lifetime, those who have been friends in sunshine and in shade. They say you are truly blessed if the fingers on your hand can name friends who have chosen to stay with you through thick and thin. I believe that some people come into our lives and quickly go, but there are a few who choose to stay for as long as there is a forever.

To this day, I can come to a place on the Meador Homestead hill and remember sharing the spot with a true friend. It may have been catching lightning bugs in a jar, drinking sweet nectar from a honeysuckle vine, discovering "dinosaur bones" and hiding them under the bed so mom wouldn't catch us sneaking out, eating banana bread and writing songs about boyfriends into the wee hours of the night, and sharing secrets knowing no one else would understand. It's flying kites, camping out, and fishing at the pond without our shirts on. Today, it's rocking and singing songs to the grandbabies, pulling weeds together in the flower beds, and of course, pouring and sipping a cup of hot tea. It's laughing, crying, and knowing that we will never be apart, maybe in distance, but never in heart.

A writer of the Victorian Era, before the cabin was even built, poetically wrote phrases so perfectly to reflect the heart of my true friends:

"Oh, the comfort, the inexpressible comfort of feeling safe with a person, having neither to weigh thoughts, nor measure words, but pouring all right out, just as they are chaff and grain together; certain that a faithful hand will take and sift them, keep what is worth keeping, and with the breath of comfort, blow the rest away." What better way to thank true friends than by honoring them with a Friends Forever Luncheon Tea? Our menu is food that can be made ahead of time, so you can spend your time with faithful friends. The food is simple, yet elegant, and sure to leave a lasting impression—like true, forever friendship!

COLD SPICED TEA

3 qts water, boiled

6 tea bags

10 whole cloves

1 stick cinnamon

Fresh mint, handful

1 ½ cups sugar

1 (6 oz) can lemonade, thawed

1 (6 oz) can orange juice, thawed

Boil water. Put tea bags, cloves, cinnamon, and mint into water. Remove from heat and let steep 15 minutes. Strain mixture into a gallon pitcher. Add sugar, stirring until dissolved. Add lemonade and orange juice. Fill container to gallon mark with water.

SHRIMP JULEP

Julep cups

Crushed ice

2 oz ramekins or sauce cups

Cocktail or remoulade sauce

Boiled shrimp, cooled

Lemon slice

Fill silver mint julep cups with ice. Place a sauce cup in the middle and fill with your favorite cocktail or remoulade sauce. Arrange shrimp around the rim of the cup.

Previous page: *Kite flying delight (1986) & Friends Forever - Sorority Sisters on the 1884 Meador Barn (1974)*
Clockwise from top left: *A butterfly's feast, this plate exudes a friendly invite, Thelma & Louise?, veggie delight, Shrimp Julep-Southern inspired*

DEVILED EGGS

2 dozen eggs, boiled and sliced

1 cup tomato soup

1 can cream of mushroom soup

1 can deviled ham

1 Tbsp chili powder

1 clove garlic

Cheddar cheese, grated

Lay boiled eggs in layers in baking dish. Mix tomato and mushroom soups, ham, chili powder, and garlic and pour over eggs. Put grated cheese over dish and heat until cheese melts.

STEAMED VEGETABLES

3 yellow squash, cut into rings

1 bunch asparagus

1 bunch broccoli

1 cup carrots, peeled

Spicy ranch dressing

Remove flesh from squash, leaving 2-inch rings. Steam each vegetable separately in boiling water and remove to a bowl of ice water to stop cooking and retain color. Place a few asparagus spears, broccoli crowns, and cooked carrots into a squash ring. Drizzle with spicy ranch dressing. Serve at room temperature. Yield: 8-10 servings.

GRILLED CHICKEN OVER ALMOND AND ORANGE GREEN SALAD

4-6 boneless, skinless chicken breasts

Lemon pepper and garlic salt

Wishbone dressing

Almond and Orange Green Salad Recipe (page 97)

Blueberries or other berries (opt)

Granny Smith apples (opt)

Salt and pepper chicken breasts and place in Ziploc bag. Pour Wishbone dressing into the bag and marinate for several hours. Grill chicken and cut into strips. Add other optional ingredients to salad if desired. Toss with dressing and place strips of grilled chicken on top. Yield: 6 to 8 servings.

BANANA BREAD

1 cup margarine

3 cups sugar

6 eggs

3 cups sour cream

4 tsp baking soda

2 tsp vanilla

5 bananas, mashed

1 tsp salt

5 cups flour

Cream butter and sugar. Mix in eggs. Mix sour cream and baking soda together in separate bowl and let stand until foamy. Combine butter mixture, sour cream mixture, vanilla, bananas, salt, and flour. Mix well. Place into greased bread pans and bake 50 minutes at 350 degrees.

From Left to Right: *Friendship - an exciting adventure, Simple never tasted so good, The ingredients of friendship last forever, Peggy and I invite you to a friendly cup of tea at Simply TeaVine*

EASY BOILED CUSTARD

1 (3.4 oz) pkg French vanilla instant pudding mix

½ cup sugar

1 tsp vanilla

4 cups milk

1 (8 oz) tub Cool Whip

1 Tbsp Apricot Brandy

Garnish:
Strawberries, blueberries, peaches, or mixed berries

Serving option without fruit:
Substitute pound cake or the Friendship Cake on facing page

Pound cake

Add pudding mix, sugar, and vanilla to milk. Stir until smooth. Fold in whipped topping. Add brandy. Chill until very, very cold. Spoon pudding into martini glasses and garnish with strawberries, blueberries, peaches, or mixed berries on top.

FRIENDSHIP CAKE

1 ½ cups Wesson oil

1 ½ cups sugar

3 eggs

3 cups self rising-flour, divided

3 cups Brandied Fruit (recipe below), well drained

2 tsp vanilla

1 cup chopped pecans

Combine oil and sugar; blend in eggs. Add 2 cups flour. Dredge fruit with remaining cup of flour and fold into batter with vanilla and pecans. Bake at 325 degrees in greased and floured tube pan for 1 hour or until done. (Watch closely the last 20 minutes so it does not burn. If necessary, turn down the temperature.)

BRANDIED FRUIT STARTER

1 cup pineapple chunks

1 cup peach slices

1 cup maraschino cherries (red and green)

1 ½ cups sugar

1 pkg dry yeast

Use a glass container with a loosely-fitting lid. Drain fruit well. Put ingredients in jar and stir with a wooden spoon until well mixed. Stir gently; don't crush fruit. Cover and let stand 2 weeks, stirring gently every few days. Do not refrigerate. Fruit is ready to use, but always save 1 cup for next batch. You add equal amounts of fruit and sugar at 2 week intervals.

A Family Gathering

Rekindling Ties with Lovin' Spoonfuls

MENU

Spinach Dip (Momma Dean) • Hot Dog Dip (Beth)

Sunshine Salad (Aline) • Broccoli Salad (Jane)

Oven-Barbecued Chicken (Patrick) • Chicken Pilaf (Cecil)

Favorite Potato Casserole (Gary) • Zesty Carrots (Edith)

Corn on the Cob • Slow Cooker Baked Beans

Coconut Cake (Otis) • Oatmeal Cookies (Nancy)

Buttermilk Fudge (Betty) • Orange Balls (Aline via Cecil)

Homemade Vanilla Ice Cream (Andrea) • Lemonade Sweet Tea

Decorations: You need a buffet-style table large enough for all the food! Paper products make clean up easy!

Our big family gatherings at the Meador Homestead cabin seemed to always be when the holidays rolled around. Cousins and their cousins would gather to give thanks for another good year, hide Easter eggs on the land, or churn the crank to deliver up the best-tasting homemade ice cream for the Fourth of July! All of this occurred as the older folks sat in the yard or around the table, laughing and telling the same tried-and-true family stories. There were colorful characters at the events such as my grandfather's first cousin, Jamie. Every holiday you could expect this 70-plus year-old man to make his presence known with the roaring of his motorcycle coming down the highway from Florence, MS, to Hattiesburg. It was loaded down with baskets or trays that he had woven as his contribution for the event. We still serve our tea on these beloved trays made by a man who didn't have much but had a talent for weaving and the biggest heart ever! Mostly, the rest of us were just plain ol' common folk. There was one common thread running through us all, however, and that was the anticipation, pride, and contentment we each felt knowing we were heading home.

There is nothing like gathering at the homestead for a family reunion. Sometimes, family gatherings are not on the home land itself but held at some close-by park, lake, or even a far-off vacation spot. No matter where it is, however, it doesn't take long for the talk to come around to the people who bind us together in one family tree. Stories of "Mama and Papa" can be retold over and over to an audience that never gets tired of hearing them. New babies with old family names are brought to show off to everyone, with the exclamation, "My, she looks just like her grandma did when she was a baby!" And, of course, tasty dishes that have been passed down from one family to another are laid out on the table, reminding us of the special person who first created the

Left: A celebration of family

delicious fare! After the blessing is given by the patriarch of the family, everyone sits down to rekindle family ties, spoonful by spoonful!

On my grandfather's 90th birthday, March 15, 1981, he wrote: "After a 'sumptuous' meal downtown, the Meador family and friends gathered at the home of Pete and Frances Meador for talk and reunion. The evening ended by a prayer and a song rendered by grandchildren representing four generations. The rendition of the song was better than any opera known to man. I thank all participants on this memorable occasion, all of whom I dearly love." C. G. (Pa) Meador

Our menu was created to make every family gathering a memorable occasion for those we love. Family favorites were named for the people who created the recipe or brought the delectable gift to a family get together. The food is to be served buffet-style, so everyone can go back for *spoonful after spoonful*.

Let's make our family gathering a place where food is the centerpiece and the main focus is on visiting. So sit back and enjoy the old and new faces. Grab a piece of candy or a cookie off the plate while the kids shoot fireworks, the women talk about their families, and the old men teach the young men how to play horseshoes.

SPINACH DIP (MOMMA DEAN)

1 (10 oz) pkg frozen spinach

1 cup mayonnaise

1 cup sour cream

1 onion, chopped

1 (8 oz) can water chestnuts, chopped

1 pkg vegetable soup dry mix (Knorr)

Melba toast

Thaw spinach but don't cook. Place on paper towels and dry. Mix all other ingredients with spinach. Cover and chill for several hours. Serve with Melba toast.

HOT DOG DIP (BETH)

1 (9 oz) jar prepared regular mustard

1 (10 oz) jar currant jelly

2 pkgs hot dogs, sliced into bite-sized pieces

Toothpicks

Mix mustard and jelly. Heat, add hot dogs, and refrigerate several hours to marinate. Heat hot dog dip again before serving with toothpicks.

Above: *A treasured family recipe;* **Below:** *The faces of family*

SUNSHINE SALAD
(ALINE)

2 cups grated carrots

1 (11 oz) can mandarin oranges, drained

1 cup pineapple chunks, drained

1 cup flaked coconut

½ cup raisins

1 (8 oz) carton sour cream

Lettuce leaves

Combine all ingredients except sour cream. Mix well and refrigerate until thoroughly chilled. Just before serving, stir in sour cream. Serve on lettuce leaf.

BROCCOLI SALAD
(JANE)

6 cups fresh broccoli florets

½ large red onion, diced

1 ¼ cup raisins

12 slices bacon, cooked crisp and crumbled

Dressing:

½ cup sugar

1 cup mayonnaise

3 Tbsp red wine vinegar

Wash broccoli and cut into pieces, if necessary. Add onions and raisins to broccoli. Place in Ziploc bag and refrigerate. Cook bacon well and crumble when cooled. For dressing, combine sugar, mayonnaise, and vinegar and mix well. Store in refrigerator. Add bacon and dressing to broccoli mixture just prior to serving.

Above: A family pleaser!; *Below:* Fun and fellowship—simply irresistable

OVEN-BARBECUED CHICKEN
(PATRICK)

4 whole chickens

Salt and pepper to taste

Barbecue sauce (recipe below)

Cut chickens into quarters. Salt and pepper to taste. Make barbecue sauce and immediately separate into two portions. Reserve Portion A to serve with cooked chicken. Coat chicken pieces with sauce from Portion B. Do not mix barbecue sauce portions, as Portion B will have touched uncooked chicken. Cover and marinate 4 hours or overnight, turning occasionally. Before putting in oven, baste with remaining sauce from Portion B. Bake at 350 degrees for 2 hours or until chicken is tender. Turn chicken frequently. Yield: 12 servings.

Sauce:
2 sticks butter

1 medium bottle steak sauce

½ bottle Worcestershire sauce

2 Tbsp onion juice

Juice and rind of 2 lemons

2 cloves garlic, grated

2 tsp sugar

Mix all ingredients and cook slowly about 15 minutes. Use sauce to marinate and baste chicken. Sauce may also be served with the cooked chicken. If the sauce is allowed to cool, it congeals and adheres to the chicken more readily.

CHICKEN PILAF
(CECIL)

1 can cream of mushroom soup

1 pkg onion soup mix

2 Tbsp pimento

¼ cup cooking sherry

1 ½ cups pre-cooked rice

4 or 5 skinless chicken breasts or chicken pieces

Pepper, garlic salt, and paprika

1 stick butter, melted

Mix mushroom soup, onion soup mix, pimento, sherry, and rice in a large, shallow, greased dish. Sprinkle skinned breasts with pepper, garlic salt, and paprika. Place chickens on rice mixture and pour 1 stick melted butter over chickens. Cover with foil and seal. Bake at 375 degrees for 2 hours.

Left & facing page top left: *Chicken-BBQ & Pilaf - family comfort food*
Top right: *Paper plates and napkins - simple is best*
Middle: *Catching up on family news*
Bottom: *All ages celebrate family*

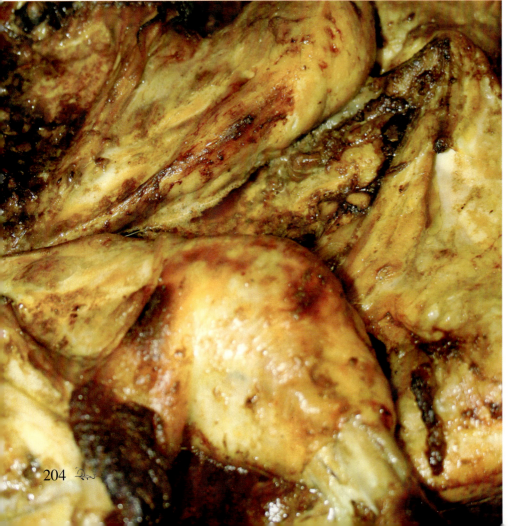

FAVORITE POTATO CASSEROLE (GARY)

1 ½ lb ground beef

1 small onion, diced

5 medium potatoes, peeled and sliced

Salt and pepper to taste

Cheese sauce:
3 Tbsp margarine

3 Tbsp flour

½ tsp salt and 1/8 tsp pepper

2 cups milk

1 ½ cups cheddar cheese grated and divided

Brown ground meat and onion. Boil potatoes until almost done. Drain potatoes and pour into a long casserole dish. In saucepan, melt margarine and flour and make a paste. Add seasonings and milk and stir until blended and thickened. Add cheese. Alternate layers of potatoes, meat, and cheese sauce. Reserve ½ cup of grated cheese and sprinkle on top. Bake at 350 degrees for 30 minutes. Yield: 10 to 12 servings.

ZESTY CARROTS
(EDITH)

6 large carrots

Boiling water

1 tsp salt

2 Tbsp grated onion

2 Tbsp prepared horseradish

½ cup mayonnaise

Salt to taste

¼ tsp pepper

¼ cup dry bread crumbs

2 Tbsp melted margarine

Peel carrots. Cut in half across the middle, then into strips. Put in medium sauce pan in boiling water to measure 1 inch. Add 1 tsp salt. Cook covered for 6 to 8 minutes or until tender. Preheat oven to 375 degrees. Drain carrots, reserving ¼ cup liquid. Pour into 10 x 6 inch (1 ½ qt) baking dish. In small bowl, combine onion, horseradish, mayonnaise, salt, pepper, and reserved liquid. Pour over carrots and spread evenly. Toss bread crumbs with margarine and sprinkle over the top. Bake at 350 degrees for 15 minutes.

CORN ON THE COB

Corn on the cob, husks and silk removed

Butter, salt, and seasonings of choice

Fill pot with water to cover corn and bring to a rolling boil. Add corn and return water to full boil. Cover pot and turn heat off. Leave pot of corn undisturbed for 10 to 15 minutes. Serve with butter and seasonings.

Clockwise from left: A family song of food, Blissfully Southern carrots, Seasonal fruit and Bubbly beans

SLOW COOKER BAKED BEANS

2 lbs ground chuck

1 large onion, chopped

6 bacon slices, cooked and crumbled

3 (16 oz) cans pork and beans

1 (12 oz) jar chili sauce

1 (8 oz) can crushed pineapple, drained

1 cup light brown sugar

1 Tbsp dry mustard

1 Tbsp Worcestershire sauce

Brown meat and onion in a large skillet, stirring until meat is done and onion is tender. Cook bacon well and crumble when cool enough to handle. Combine meat mixture, bacon, pork and beans, and remaining ingredients in a 4 quart slow cooker, stirring well. Cover and cook on high for 3 ½ hours. Yield: 10 servings.

COCONUT CAKE (OTIS)

⅔ cup shortening

2 cups sugar

3 cups sifted cake flour

3 tsp baking powder

½ tsp salt

1 cup milk

1 tsp vanilla

5 egg whites, stiffly beaten

Coconut milk

Cream shortening. Add sugar gradually and cream until light and fluffy. Mix dry ingredients and add alternately with milk and vanilla to creamed mixture. Fold stiffly beaten egg whites into batter. Pour into 2 greased 9-inch round cake pans and bake at 350 degrees for 30 minutes. Pour coconut milk over cake when you take it out and it will be moist. Make frosting and spread over cake when cool.

Boiled Frosting

1 cup sugar

½ cup water

3 egg whites

1 tsp vanilla

Cook the sugar and water together stirring until the sugar has dissolved. Take from heat and without stirring, allow to cool. Beat egg whites stiff. Pour the syrup in a thin stream over the egg whites, beating the mixture constantly until thick enough to spread. Add vanilla and spread over layers.

*The consumption of raw or undercooked eggs may increase your risk of food-borne illness, especially to children and the elderly.

OATMEAL COOKIES
(NANCY)

¾ cup shortening, soft

¾ cup firmly packed brown sugar

¾ cup granulated sugar

1 egg

¼ cup water

1 tsp vanilla

1 ¼ cups all-purpose flour

1 tsp salt

½ tsp baking soda

2 ½ cups old-fashioned oats

1 cup chopped pecans

Beat together: shortening, sugars, egg, water, and vanilla until creamy. Sift together: flour, salt, and baking soda. Add to creamed mixture; blend well. Stir in oats and pecans. Drop by teaspoonfuls onto greased cookie sheets. Bake in preheated oven at 350 degrees for 12 to 15 minutes. Yield: 4 dozen cookies.

BUTTERMILK FUDGE
(BETTY)

2 cups sugar

1 cup buttermilk

¼ cup butter

½ tsp baking soda

2 Tbsp white corn syrup

A lot of pecans, chopped (opt)

1 tsp vanilla

Mix first 5 ingredients and heat over medium heat in a large pot until it comes to a boil and thickens. Set off heat and add pecans and vanilla. When lukewarm, beat until thick as for fudge. Pour out into buttered plate. This candy turns a rich brown before your eyes!

ORANGE BALLS
(ALINE'S VIA CECIL)

1 box powdered sugar

1 stick margarine, softened

1 small box vanilla wafers, crushed

2 cups, finely chopped nuts

1 (6 oz) can frozen orange juice

Powdered sugar or coconut flakes to roll in

Mix powdered sugar and margarine that has been softened with vanilla wafers, nuts, and orange juice. Mix with hands or use a blender. Roll dough into balls any size you wish! Roll into coconut flakes or powdered sugar.

HOMEMADE VANILLA ICE CREAM
(ANDREA)

4 eggs, beaten

1 2/3 cup sugar

Dash of salt

2 Tbsp vanilla

1 tall can evaporated milk

1 can condensed milk

Whole milk

1 can crushed pineapple (opt)

1 pint peaches (opt)

Strawberries or figs (opt)

Start with eggs in mixer. Beat until creamy. Add sugar and beat. Add salt and vanilla. Add evaporated and condensed milks. Pour in ice cream maker and fill rest of container with milk. Freeze in an electric ice cream maker.

Variations: A can of crushed pineapple, a pint of peaches, strawberries, or figs may be added in ice cream maker if desired.

*The consumption of raw or undercooked eggs may increase your risk of food-borne illness, especially to children and the elderly.

LEMONADE SWEET TEA

3 cups water

2 family-size tea bags

1 cup fresh mint leaves

1/2 cup sugar

4 cups cold water

1/2 (12 oz) can frozen lemonade concentrate, thawed

Bring 3 cups water to a boil. Remove from heat and add tea bags and mint. Cover and steep for 10 minutes. Discard tea bags and mint. Stir in sugar until dissolved. Pour tea into a container and stir in 4 cups of cold water and lemonade concentrate. Serve over ice.

All Left: Sugar, Spice, and Sweet Tea

"March 21, 1971 ~ Today, my immediate family met again and enjoyed another "bountiful" meal prepared by my wife, Jessie. Miss Dean returned thanks with a beautiful little prayer, which, unbeknown to her, touched the bottom of my heart."   C. G. (Pa) Meador

Top Left: C.G. Meador's 90th birthday! (1981)
All the rest: Laughter, food, and fellowship - the essentials of family

Sewing Circle
and Southern Sides
(A Luncheon with Special Friends)

MENU

Pam's Artichoke Dip

Dean's Appleade Fizz

Jan's Hot Chicken Salad

Katherine's Vegetable Salad

Refrigerator Rolls

Marsha's Peach-Berry Compote

Kit's Fudge Sundae Pie

Decorations: We used a family handmade quilt for our tablecloth. Hand-stitched handkerchiefs tied with ribbon were used as napkins, and small framed samplers and sewing accoutrements adorned the table. For place cards and favors, buy small mending kits and personalize.

In a corner of the 1884 cabin, the original family spinning wheel sits proudly worn, a glorious tribute to the fortitude and courage of the women who once graced this home. My great, great grandmother's rocking chair sits beside it, and images of her working the wheel with determination flow through my mind. This would have been one of the main items a woman would have brought, if nothing else, when they settled into a new home. In another corner sits the Singer sewing machine that dates, according to its serial number, 1915 and to another time. Thread has been left on both, almost as if work has been interrupted to welcome a traveling guest into the home to stay for the night. In the same room, a tulip quilt, made by my grandmother years later, rests caresses the baby bed. It is this uncommon thread of sewing that has brought women of all generations together.

Meador Homestead is a dogtrot cabin and was built so a breeze will constantly blow through the passageway between the two rooms. It is in this open hallway where most of the domestic chores were done and where the women would have gathered to escape the Mississippi heat. They would churn the milk to make butter, shell the peas for the next meal, sew, and tell of their lives, giving support to one another.

The years fast forward to 1987, and I sit with my "sewing circle." No spinning wheels around, no sewing machines—only a few cross-stitched samplers and needles patching torn jeans. We gather together mainly not to sew, but to slip into a place of camaraderie, deep loyalty, and love. It is an outlet from the normal and ordinary. We share our child-rearing secrets, our hopes and sorrows, and, of course, our recipes with each other, just like our ancestors did before. We have found the uncommon thread of sewing that ties us together and as we listen and talk, our hearts are engaged in something very extraordinary and unusual—true kindred spirits.

An anonymous poem, "The Sewing Circle, its design, deeds, and prospects," written in 1850, describe the benefit of these meetings: "It is for social intercourse we meet/And each with kindly sympathies to greet./Discordant feelings all to lay aside/For suffer might our unity divide….The longest life; at best, but one short span,/Then for each other, let's do what we can."

This menu includes some of the Southern recipes I enjoyed with my sewing-circle friends. The fellowship and the food are my favorite memories from these exceptional sisters. Honor your group of special friends with a Sewing Circle Luncheon. No threads need be around for the common thread of friendship.

PAM'S ARTICHOKE DIP

6-8 oz Parmesan cheese (buy in wedge)

1 (14 oz) can artichoke hearts, drained

1 cup mayonnaise

Cayenne, Tabasco, and salt for seasonings

Crackers or pita bread triangles

Cut cheese into cubes and melt in microwave. Add artichokes and mayonnaise. Add seasonings and heat to serve. Serve with plain crackers or pita bread triangles. Serves 15.

DEAN'S APPLEADE FIZZ

3 cups apple juice or cider

⅓ cup lemon juice

⅓ cup lime juice

⅓ cup sugar

Crushed ice and ice cubes

Club soda

Shake all ingredients except club soda with crushed ice and strain over ice cubes into glasses. Fill with soda. Yields: 8 servings.

JAN'S HOT CHICKEN SALAD

3 cups diced (not too small) cooked chicken

2 cans (4 ½ oz) chopped olives

1 can (8 oz) drained mushrooms

¼ cup chopped onions

½ cup mayonnaise

1 can cream of chicken soup, undiluted

1 cup sour cream (8 oz)

6 slices white bread, cubed

Sprinkle of Lea & Perrins

Worcestershire Sauce

Pepper

Prep all ingredients, mix, and place in shallow 8 x 10 baking dish. Cover with foil and refrigerate overnight. The next day, bake 1 hour at 300 degrees. Cover with foil while baking. Remove foil for the last 20 minutes.

Previous page: Old tools of the trade
Clockwise from left: 19th Century Spinning Wheel, 1913 Singer, Hand-sewn cozy & sampler, Fizzy drink and hot chicken salad - "sewcial" therapy!

KATHERINE'S VEGETABLE SALAD

1 cup cauliflower florets

1 cup sliced carrots

1 cup sliced mushrooms

1 cup sliced Brussels sprouts

1 cup sliced yellow squash

1 cup broccoli florets

1 ½ cup sliced zucchini

½ cup sliced radishes

Dressing:
¾ cup lemon juice

¾ cup vegetable oil

3 Tbsp sugar

½ tsp pepper

1 ½ tsp oregano

1 Tbsp salt

Prep and combine 7 of the vegetables, holding radishes in reserve. In a separate small bowl, mix all dressing ingredients until well blended. Pour dressing over vegetable mixture and toss. Marinate in refrigerator for 24 hours. Just before serving, add ½ cup radishes.

Food: *The intricate design of vegetable salad, Pie and compote - finishing touches to a masterpiece meal*

Sewing Essentials: *Original thread left on spinning wheel, antique iron & sewing thread, A perfect place card (sewing kit), Creating an heirloom work*

REFRIGERATOR ROLLS

1 package dry yeast

¼ cup warm water

1 cup shortening

½ cup sugar

3 eggs, lightly beaten

1 cup warm milk

1 tsp salt

5 cups all-purpose flour

⅓ cup butter, melted

Dissolve yeast in warm water; set aside. In mixing bowl, cream shortening; gradually add sugar and beat until light and fluffy. Stir in eggs, milk, and yeast mixture; beat until smooth. Stir in salt and flour to make a sticky dough. Place dough in a well greased bowl, turning to grease top. Cover and refrigerate 24 hours. Remove dough from refrigerator 2 hours before serving. Lightly grease standard muffin pans. Punch dough down and shape into 1 inch balls. Place 3 balls in each muffin cup. Cover and let rise in a warm place, free from drafts, 1 hour or until doubled in bulk. Bake at 400 degrees for 12 minutes or until light brown. Brush with butter and serve hot. Yield: 3 dozen rolls

MARSHA'S PEACH-BERRY COMPOTE

5 large ripe peaches, peeled and sliced

1 cup fresh blueberries or frozen, thawed

1 cup fresh raspberries or frozen, thawed

⅔ cup granulated sugar

6 to 8 fresh mint leaves

Sweetened whipped cream (opt)

Place peaches and blueberries in dish. Mash raspberries through a sieve. Combine raspberries and sugar in blender, and blend for 3 minutes. Pour puree over fruit. Bake at 350 degrees for 12 minutes; cool and refrigerate. Do not stir until ready to serve. Spoon into individual serving bowls and top with fresh mint leaves. Yield: 6 to 8 servings. You can top with sweetened whipped cream to serve as a dessert.

KIT'S FUDGE SUNDAE PIE

1 cup evaporated milk

1 (6 oz) pkg semisweet chocolate chips

1 cup miniature marshmallows

¼ tsp salt

Vanilla wafers

Quart of vanilla ice cream

Whole pecans

Put milk, chips, marshmallow, and salt in heavy saucepan and stir over medium heat until melted and thickened. Take off heat and cool to room temperature. Line bottom of a 9-inch pie pan with vanilla wafers. Spoon half of a quart of vanilla ice cream over the wafers. Cover with half of chocolate. Repeat with rest of ice cream and then, the rest of the chocolate. Put whole pecans on top and freeze until firm. Remove from freezer 15 to 20 minutes before ready to serve.

INDEX

Appetizers and Dips
Asparagus Chantilly, 49
Black-Eyed Pea Dip, 92
Cheese Bake Dip, 121
Cynthia's Family Reunion Dip, 84
Hot Dog Dip (Beth), 202
John Buckley's Shrimp Dip, 182
Mini Sausage Rolls, 49
Nancy's Cheese Ring, 148
Nancy's Fruit and Fruit Dip, 85
Pam's Artichoke Dip, 214
Sausage Balls, 122
Spinach Dip (Momma Dean), 202

Beverages
Blackberry Sweet Tea, 59
Champagne Punch from Old Southern Tea Room, 104
Champagne Punch, 130
Cold Spiced Tea, 196
Dean's Appleade Fizz, 215
Evelyn's Banana Punch, 32
Ginger and Honey Sweet Tea, 92
Lemonade Sweet Tea, 209
Lemon Blueberry Sweet Tea, 63
Mint Julep Sweet Tea, 185
Famous Mint Julep from Old Southern Tea Room, 104
Peach Tea Punch with Simple Sugar, 25
Plantation Iced Tea, 105
Slushy Punch, 42
Southern Sweet Tea, 193
Wassail, 123

Breads and Rolls
Banana Bread, 198
Basic Scones, 43
Buttermilk Cornbread, 111
Chai Tea Mini Biscuits, 39
Cinnamon Pecan Rolls, 177
Cloverleaf Refrigerator Rolls, 168
Cornbread Dressing, 118
Effie's Apple Muffins, 179
Elizabeth's Biscuits, 34
English Muffin French Toast, 178
French Market Doughnuts, 17
Herbed Crescent Rolls, 150
Hoecakes, 143
Iron Skillet Cornbread, 100
Italian Breadsticks, 64
Lavender and Honey Scones, 51
Parmesan Cheese Breadsticks, 184
Pecan Pie Muffins, 76
Pecan Waffles, 176
Quick Buttermilk Biscuits, 177
Refrigerator Rolls, 217
Simple French Toast, 179
Sweet Potato Biscuits, 129
Whole Grain Pan Rolls, 189
Zucchini Bread, 59

Cakes
Blueberry Cheesecake, 79
Carrot Cake Muffins, 41
Checkerboard Cake, 192
Chocolate Fudge Cupcakes, 87
Chocolate Round Pound Cake, 137
Coca Cola Cake, 43
Coconut Cake (Otis), 207
Election or "Rum Cake", 104
Friendship Cake, 199
Heavenly Hash Cake, 144
Hummingbird Cake, 143
Lady Baltimore Cake, 136
Petit Four Wedding Cakes, 51
Sour Cream Coffee Cake, 178
Toll House Cupcakes, 191
Turbinado Strawberry Shortcakes with Cream, 96
Westminster Abbey Chocolate Hat Cake, 52
Yellow Cake with Caramel Icing, 122

Casseroles
Asparagus Casserole, 121
Cottage Pie, 49
Creole Breakfast Bread Pudding, 175
Eggplant Zucchini Parmigiana, 66
Favorite Potato Casserole (Gary), 205
Grandmother's Sweet Potato Casserole, 26
Green Bean Casserole, 190
Meat Lasagna, 64
Squash Casserole, 27
Tuna Fish Casserole, 189

Cheese
Brie en Croute, 24
Cheese Delights, 93
Nancy's Cheese Ring, 148

Candy
Buttermilk Fudge (Betty), 208
Iron Skillet Fudge Candy, 160

Cookies
$250 Cookie Recipe, 40
Chocolate Nut Clusters, 123
Ms. Lena's Sugar Cookies, 191
Oatmeal Cookies (Nancy), 208
Orange Balls (Aline's via Cecil), 209
Spud's Cocoons, 169
Sweetheart Sugar Cookies, 40
Wedding Cake Cookies with Frosting, 52
White Chocolate Pretzels, 39

Desserts
Ambrosia, 168
Bananas Foster, 21
Beehives, 67
Blackberry Cobbler, 58
Christmas Delight, 122
Cynthia's Blueberry Tart, 160
Easy Boiled Custard, 198
Frosty Strawberry Squares, 29
Homemade Vanilla Ice Cream (Andrea), 209
Luscious Lemon Squares, 71
Miniature Cheesecakes, 53
Peach Cobbler, 113
Peach Crisp, 137
Peach Melba, 53
Skillet Peaches `a la Mode, 159
White Chocolate Mousse with Strawberries, 169

Eggs
Deviled Eggs, 197
Eggs Benedict, 18
Erin's Stuffed Eggs, 87

Fruit
Brandied Fruit Starter, 199
Buttery Cinnamon Skillet Apples, 179
Decadent Cherries, 151
Figs Wrapped in Prosciutto, 63
Fresh Fruit with Dressing, 94
Fruit in Orange Cup, 16
Mandarin Oranges and Grapes, 133
Marsha's Peach-Berry Compote, 217
Mixed Berries, 111
Pineapple and Blackberries, 78
Strawberries and Balsamic Vinegar, 64
Stuffed Strawberries with Crème, 50

Icings
Basic Decorator Icing, 52
Boiled Frosting, 207
Caramel Icing, 122
Chocolate Butter Icing, 192
Coca Cola Cake Frosting, 43
Cream Cheese Frosting, 143
Cream Cheese Icing, 41
Fondant Icing, 51

Meat
Beef with Sour Cream, 156
Boston Butt Pork Roast, 26
Cheeseburger in Paradise, 111
Corned Beef and Cabbage, 131
Country Fried Steak with Gravy, 157
Marinated Beef Tenderloin, 166

Pies
$100 Fudge Pie, 150
Andrea's Pineapple Cream Pie, 35
Chess Pie with Blackberries, 86
Chocolate Pie, 185
Georgia's Pecan Pie, 101
Iron Skillet Apple Pie, 158
Kit's Fudge Sundae Pie, 217
Lemon Iced Box Pie, 112
Old Virginia Sweet Potato Pie, 103
Pumpkin Pie, 123
Strawberry Pie, 28
Tomato Pie, 56
Weidmann's Blackbottom Pie, 193

Pork
"Apple a Day" Pork Chops, 133
Country Ham with Redeye Gravy, 176
Honey Baked Ham, 101
Pork Chops Creole, 156

Poultry-Chicken, Quail, Turkey
Barbecued Chicken, 110
Chicken Pilaf (Cecil), 204
Fricasseed Chicken over Rice, 103
Jan's Hot Chicken Salad, 215
Mom's Easy Chicken, 35
Oven-Barbecued Chicken (Patrick), 204
Paradise Chicken Salad on Croissant, 93
Smothered Quail, 188
Southern Fried Chicken, 86
Turkey in a Bag, 117

Salads
Almond and Orange Green Salad, 95
Asian Coleslaw, 118
Broccoli Salad (Jane), 203
Caesar Iceberg Wedges, 184
Cranberry Salad, 191
Garden Salad with Russian Dressing, 25
Grandmother's Apricot Congealed Salad, 32
Grilled Chicken over Almond and Orange Green Salad, 197
Katherine's Vegetable Salad, 216
Panzanella Salad with Cornbread Croutons, 63
Salmon Green Salad with Aioli Sauce, 165
Smoky Blue Cheese Cabbage Slaw, 134
Smoky Sweet Potato Salad, 71
Spinach and Strawberry Daiquiri Salad, 78
Strawberry Congealed Salad, 148
Sunshine Salad (Aline), 203
Winter Apple Salad, 140

Sandwiches
Cucumber Benedictine Sandwich, 42
Dad's Pimento and Cheese, 85
Fried Green Tomato B.L.T., 70
Fried Peanut Butter and Banana Sandwich, 108
Grilled Apple and Cheese Sandwich, 142
Smoked Salmon, 48
Turkey, Bacon, and Muenster Sandwich, 141
Waldorf Sandwich, 38

Sauces, Syrups, and Creams
Aioli Sauce, 165
Barbecued Chicken Sauce, 110
Chantilly Crème, 49
Blender Hollandaise Sauce, 18
Clotted Crème, 39
Crabapple Jelly, 39
Curry Vegetable Dip, 85
Fruit Dip, 85
Fruit Salad Dressing, 94
Giblet Gravy, 117
Hard Sauce, 67
Lemon Curd, 39
Oven Barbecued Chicken Sauce, 204
Pear Preserves, 174
Raspberry Sauce, 53
Redeye Gravy, 176
Remoulade Sauce, 70
Russian Dressing, 25
Shrimp Sauce, 77
Simple Sugar, 25

Seafood
Broiled Shrimp, 132
Crab Crepes with Shrimp Sauce, 77
John Buckley's Shrimp Dip, 182
Shrimp Eudora, 109
Shrimp Julep, 196

Soups
Beef and Vegetable Soup, 149
Chicken Noodle Soup, 154
Chili, 110
Crabmeat Bisque, 101
Homemade Vegetable and Beef Soup, 155
Italian Bread Soup, 164
Minestrone Soup, 65
Navy Bean Soup, 188
New Year's Day Soup, 135
Potato and Corn Chowder, 141
Preacher Man's Stew, 142
Rusty's Gumbo, 183
Skillet Orange Chili Chicken, 154
Slow-Cooked Chili, 120
Vichyssoise, 73

Vegetables & Sides
Black-Eyed Peas—Plantation Style, 102
Broccoli Casserole, 167
Brussels Sprouts, 56
Buttered Peas, 101
Copper Pennies, 129
Corn on the Cob, 206
Creamy Grits, 176
Dean's Twice-Baked Potatoes, 33
Fried Green Beans, 66
Fried Squash, 57
Grandmother's Sweet Potato Casserole, 26
Green Bean Casserole, 190
Grilled Asparagus, 19
Grits Martini, 20
Hoppin' John, 134
Mashed Potatoes with Cheese, 167
Nancy's Green Beans with Catalina, 34
Old Southern "Cawn Puddin," 100
Peggy's Squash Soufflé, 33
Red Rice, 189
Skillet Asparagus with Tomato Slice, 78
Slow Cooker Baked Beans, 207
Southern Peas, 190
Squash Casserole, 27
Squaw Corn, 120
Steamed Broccoli, 149
Steamed Vegetables, 197
Sweet Potato Fries, 129
Turnip Greens, 100, 131
Vegetables and Curry Vegetable Dip, 85
Veggie Chips, 70
Zesty Carrots (Edith), 206

Credit Recipes

Ms Sippy (Simply TeaVine Cookbook), Old Vicksburg Wedding Reception Cookbook , Old Southern Tea Room Cookbook, Brennans restaurant in New Orleans, Weidmanns restaurant in Meridian, The First Ladies Cookbook

Jane Boudreaux
Betty Brockman
Louise Brown
John Buckley
Peggy Bullion
Otis Caperton
Jere Clark
Cecil Clements
JoAnn Covington
Aline Darby
Edith Davis
Sandra Davis
Erin Dornan
Cynthia Easterling
Rusty Ellis
Nancy Meador Farrar
Elizabeth Garner
Glenda Grubbs
Wanda Harden
Dr. Emily Harden
Carol Harrison
Jackie Hedgepeth
Katherine Holliman
Cynthia Holmes
June Hunt
Doris James
Ann Johnson
Andrea Jussely
Marsha Lambert
Ruby Lipe
Queen Mackey
Lorene Mangum
Nancy McKee

Janet McLelland
Beth Steadman Meador
Jessie Green Meador
Mary Celina Arnold Meador
Georgia Miller
Mrs. Powell Ogletree
Ame Phelps
Janet Poole
Pam Rouse
Kit Saliba
Edie Sigrest
Jeff Sims
Dean Meador Smith
Pauline Smith
Nannie Beth Steadman
Jan Tatum
Phyllis Thomas
Evelyn Wesley

Other Credits

Cover & Jacket Design: Jason Kauffmann

Front Cover Photographs: Corey Lunsford

Back Cover Drawing: Janet Payne Walker

Interior Design: Michael Covington

Interior Editing: Adam Tillinghast & Donna Melillo

Photography: Eddie and Dean Smith, Adams Garner, Joanna Holbert, (Chi Omega Sorority picture from McCain Library and Archives, University of Southern Mississippi), Michael Covington

Quotations and Writings: C. G. Meador (Pa), excerpt from Stepping Heavenward by Mrs. E. Prentiss, the poem "Walk the Woods" by Glen Smith, song "Evening in December" by Tricia Walker of Big Front Productions, Levi Parks Meador's license to preach in the Methodist Episcopal Church South, Methodist minister Pierce Harris, Pauline Smith (Eddie's mom), Wyse.

Goodbye All...

"Hope you feel thoroughly satisfied…"

"…next time you are rolling through, don't forget to stop and rest…"

"…we'll leave the light on for you."